## POCKET

# MILAN

### TOP EXPERIENCES · LOCAL LIFE

T0018251

**PAULA HARDY**

# Contents

## Plan Your Trip

## Special Features

The original Prada store
CASIMIRO PT/SHUTTERSTOCK ©

## Explore Milan 29

## Worth a Trip

## Survival Guide 145

### COVID-19

We have re-checked every business in this book before publication to ensure that it is still open after the COVID-19 outbreak. However, the economic and social impacts of COVID-19 will continue to be felt long after the outbreak has been contained, and many businesses, services and events referenced in this guide may experience ongoing restrictions. Some businesses may be temporarily closed, have changed their opening hours and services, or require bookings; some will unfortunately have closed their doors permanently. We suggest you check with venues before visiting for the latest information.

# Milan's Top Experiences

## Climb to the Roof of the Duomo (p32)

**Admire Leonardo da Vinci's Last Supper (p98)**

**Wander the Masterpiece-Packed Halls of Pinacoteca di Brera (p72)**

**Get Arty at Museo del Novecento (p36)**

# Explore History at Castello Sforzesco (p70)

Journey to the Borromean Islands (p134)

# Discover Renaissance Artworks at Museo Poldi Pezzoli (p50)

LESTERTAIRSHUTTERSTOCK ©

**Explore the Museo Nazionale Scienza e Tecnologia (p100)**

# Dining Out

*Milan's dining scene is like its fashion scene, with restaurant openings hotly debated and Michelin-starred tables hard to come by. Milanese cooking is influenced by French and Austrian traditions, in addition to which the city offers a wealth of regional Italian and ethnic eateries. Make reservations Friday through Sunday.*

## Food History

Northern Italian food is city food originating from one of the richest urban cultures on the planet. Peasants may have toiled in the fields, but they rarely had the means to eat anything more exciting than wild garlic, greens and polenta. The people with the real knowledge to transform the country's growing abundance of ingredients were the inhabitants of wealthy cities like Milan. As Venetian and Genoese sailors offloaded their cargoes of spices, sugar, saffron, fruit, citrus and nuts from around the Mediterranean, so traders distributed them via northern Italy's navigable network of rivers. Powerful clans like Milan's Sforza's competed for a slice of the profits, taxing trade and patronising the best cooks of the day. It was in this competitive commercial environment that Italy's great cuisine was born.

## Foreign Flavours

Milan's generations of internal Italian immigrants have injected the cuisine of virtually every region into the lifeblood of the city, where you'll often find Genovese, Piedmontese and Tuscan dishes sharing menu space with local Lombard classics. As well as the food of these near neighbours, Milan's increasingly diverse global population is also reflected in the city's eating habits. Unusually for Italy, Japanese and Chinese restaurants are commonplace and the cuisines of India, the Middle East, sub-Saharan Africa and, most recently, Latin America are all represented.

KOKOPHOTOS/SHUTTERSTOCK ©

## Best Milanese

**Ratanà** A native Milanese chef turns out some of the city's best local cuisine. (p90)

**Latteria di San Marco** A classic family concern dishing up Milanese home cooking. (p79)

**Trattoria Milanese** Old-school restaurant in a pretty cobbled street. (p42)

**Luini** The oldest *panzerotti* (savoury pastry) take-away in the city. (p41)

## Best Regional Italian

**Ristorante da Giacomo** Classic Tuscan seafood dishes in an elegant Mongiardino-designed restaurant. (p131)

**A Santa Lucia** A Neapolitan restaurant with a celebrated history. (p41)

**Volemose Bene** Taste the punchy flavours of the south in this raucous Roman trattoria. (p79)

**Trattoria del Pescatore** Outstanding Sardinian cuisine, including the best lobster in town. (p128)

## Best Ethnic Eateries

**Tokuyoshi** Michelin-starred Italian-Japanese cuisine with a refined aesthetic. (p117)

**Casa Ramen Super** An Italian take on ramen that stays true to the soul of the dish. (p89)

**Dim Sum** Chinese cuisine showcasing Lombard ingredients. (p58)

**NÚN** Reinvents the humble Middle Eastern kebab as gourmet wraps. (p57)

## Best Michelin Stars

**Ristorante Berton** Food that pushes the boundaries to produce 'evolved' Italian cuisine. (p90)

**Seta** One of the most talked-about dining destinations in town. (p80)

**Cracco** Deconstructive *alta cucina* from Milan's most famous chef. (pictured above; p42)

**Alice Ristorante** Viviana Varese's exciting contemporary restaurant in Eataly's flagship store. (p92)

# Bar Open

*Drinking is a stylish affair in Milan and an opportunity for la bella figura (making a good impression). Cocktail and wine bars abound, particularly in Navigli, Porta Romana and Isola, and stay open until 2am, while clubs are open until 5am. Zero's (http://zero.eu/milano) fortnightly guide and info is useful, as is 2night (http://2night.it/milano).*

## Aperitivo

Happy hour elsewhere in the world might mean downing cut-price pints and stale crisps, but not in oh-so-stylish Milan. Its nightly *aperitivo* (predinner drinks with snacks) is a two- or three-hour ritual, starting around 6pm, where for €8 to €20, a cocktail, glass of wine, or beer comes with an unlimited buffet of bruschetta, foccacia, cured meats, salads, and even seafood and pasta. (Occasionally you'll pay a cover charge up front that includes a drink and buffet fare, which generally works out the same.) Take a plate and help yourself; snacks are also sometimes brought to your table. Most of the city's bars offer *aperitivi*, in some form or other.

## Best Cocktails

**Mag Cafè** Creative cocktails in a laid-back canalside bar with a speakeasy vibe. (pictured above; p119)

**Bar Rita** An American-style cocktail bar serving up the classics with a twist. (p119)

**Bamboo Bar** The best designer bar in the city. (p60)

**Bar Basso** A Milanese institution and the home of the negroni *sbagliato*. (p61)

**Octavius Bar** Top cocktails by a one-time barman of the year. (p93)

**Botanical Club** Fabulous gin-based cocktails from Milan's first microdistillery. (p93)

## Best Historic Cafes

**Pasticceria Marchesi** Serving coffee and superlative cakes beneath historic painted ceilings since 1824. (p105)

**Pasticceria Cova** Milan's oldest cafe, opened in 1817 by Antonio Cova, a soldier of Napoleon. (p53)

**Gattullo** Perfect coffee and pastries from southern baking impresario Joseph Gattullo. (p113)

KEVIN FAINGNAERT/LONELY PLANET ©

**Pasticceria Cucchi** 1930s style and a devilish raspberry pie. (p116)

**Sant'Ambroeus** Opened by French pastry chefs in the belle époque and famous for its pralines. (p61)

## Best Wine Bars

**Cantine Isola** One of the few places you can taste top-shelf producers by the glass. (p92)

**Vinoir** A youthful crew and an interesting list of biodynamic wines. (p118)

**Ricerca Vini** A restaurant and wine vendor with a huge and well-curated inventory. (p106)

**N'Ombra de Vin** All-day tastings in a former Augustinian refectory. (p81)

## Best Aperitivo

**Ceresio 7** A rooftop perch with stylish snacks to match the views. (p93)

**Cantine Isola** Lovingly prepared snacks to pair with top-quality wines. (p92)

**Pasticceria Marchesi** A picture-perfect *spritz* (cocktail made with *prosecco*) with pretty snacks to match. (p60)

**oTTo** Scandi smørrebrøds (open sandwiches) and a hipster crowd. (p92)

**Frida** Fun people-watching and over 80 cocktails, beers and wines to choose from. (p93)

**Dry** Why bother with a buffet when this bar pairs cocktails with perfect pizzas? (p81)

## Best Night Out

**Apollo Club** A vintage-style bar with dinner, dancing and international DJs. (p113)

**Santeria Social Club** An ex-Volvo dealership turned cultural venue and live-music hub. (p132)

**VOLT** Fashion-forward club vying that takes its cool cue from Berlin. (p118)

**Alcatraz** A huge club featuring Latino, house and classic rock 'n' roll. (p93)

**Nidaba Theatre** An award-winning live-music venue hosting serious blues, soul and folk. (p120)

# Treasure Hunt

*Milan is an industry town that lives and breathes fashion and design and takes retail as seriously as it does biotech or engineering. Beyond the heart-fluttering price tags of the the Quadrilatero (the Quad), the rest of the city abounds with vintage stores, concept shops, multibrand retailers, cute boutiques and artisanal ateliers.*

## Where to Shop

Beyond the dazzling big-name brands in the Quad, there are a wealth of other shopping experiences to be had in Milan. Younger labels and a hip new breed of multibrand retailers can be found in Brera, Corso Como, Corso Magenta, Corso di Porta Ticinese and Navigli, while midrange labels and chains line bustling Via Torino, Corso Vercelli and Corso Buenos Aires. Milan's interior and industrial designers have showrooms throughout the city, although many concentrate in the streets surrounding Piazza San Babila.

## Tax Refunds

Non-EU residents spending more than €155 can claim a refund when they depart the EU. The refund only applies to purchases from retail outlets that display a 'tax-free for tourists' sign. You can claim your refund at the airport or at any office of Global Blue (www.globalblue.com) or Premier Tax Free (https://premiertaxfree.com).

## Best Shopping Experiences

**Quadrilatero d'Oro** The world's most famous luxury shopping quarter. (p67)

**NonostanteMarras** Milan's most creative concept store. (p123)

**Spazio Rossana Orlandi** Creative design and homewares in a former tie factory. (p108)

**10 Corso Como** Cutting-edge fashion from Carla Sozzani. (p95)

## Best Heritage Brands

**Borsalino** Maker of the world's coolest hats for more than 150 years. (p63)

ALEXANDRE ROTENBERG/SHUTTERSTOCK ©

**Pellini** Costume jewellery from the granddaughters of a La Scala costumier. (p108)

**Aspesi** Understated, stylish outdoor gear and leisurewear. (p62)

**F. Pettinaroli** Monogrammed stationery for top desk dressing. (p82)

**Foto Veneta Ottica** 1930s photo studio filled with supercool sunnies. (p120)

## Best for Food & Wine

**Peck** Crammed with every delectable Milanese treat you can imagine. (p44)

**Eataly** A multistorey temple of gastronomic goodness. (pictured above; p92)

**Zaini** The original Milanese chocolates wrapped like Christmas presents. (p95)

**Cantine Isola** An impressive array of hard-to-find regional wines. (p92)

## Best Vintage Finds

**Cavalli e Nastri** Early- and mid-20th-century Italian fashion-house names. (p82)

**Mania Vintage** Authenticated bags and accessories from the most coveted brands. (p133)

**Il Cirmolo** A treasure trove of homewares and collectable artefacts. (p82)

## Best Stylist's Eye

**Biffi** Edgier pieces curated with a hyper-fashionable sensibility. (p120)

**Imarika** Bold colours and prints are given a modern Milanese make-over. (p63)

**Slowear Store** Timeless menswear supported by an ethical philosophy. (p83)

**Wait and See** Eclectic, super-fun, highly wearable collection. (p45)

**Dictionary** Elegant streetwear delivering a sharp contemporary look. (p121)

# Art

*Milan's museums contain collections to rival any in Italy, with works from the Middle Ages through to modernist masters. What's more, you can often linger with a Bellini or Caravaggio without the usual crowds, even in Milan's most famous gallery, the Pinacoteca di Brera. The city is also a treasure trove of 20th-century art.*

## Enlightened Vision

The great museum tradition for which Milan is famous can be traced back to the educational aims of Counter-Reformation cardinal, Federico Borromeo (1564–1631). During his 36 years as Milan's cardinal, he distinguished himself through his incorruptible virtue, academic zeal and civic patronage. In 1609 he founded the Biblioteca Ambrosiana, which along with Oxford's Bodleian, was one of the first public libraries in Europe. In 1618 he also donated his art collection to the Ambrosian academy and laid the foundation of a public institution that could work with the school training artists.

## The Contemporary Scene

Milan's creative reputation is usually linked to the fashion and design industry, but the city's contemporary art scene is, with neighbouring Turin, the most dynamic in Italy. The majority of Italy's living artists choose to call Milan home, at least between sojourns in New York or Berlin, while Milan's annual art fair, Miart (www.miart.it) is the largest in Italy, attracting more than 45,000 visitors and 200 exhibitors.

## Best Frescoes

**The Last Supper** (p98)
Not strictly a fresco at all; Leonardo da Vinci's *The Last Supper* breaks all the rules.

**Chiesa di San Maurizio**
Seventy years in the making, San Maurizio's frescoes still dazzle onlookers. (p103)

S74/SHUTTERSTOCK ©

**Basilica di Sant'Eustorgio**
At the heart of this basilica
is the lovely Portinari Chapel
decorated by Renaissance
great, Vincenzo Foppa.
(p115)

**Chiesa di Santa Maria
Presso di San Satiro** San
Satiro's tiny chapel made
large with Bramante's
brilliant *trompe l'oeil* niche.
(p40)

## Best Period
Collections

**Castello Sforzesco** A
collection spanning the
city's history and including Michelangelo's moving
*Rondanini Pietà*. (p70)

**Pinacoteca di Brera** A stag-
gering roll-call of masters
from Titian and Tintoretto to
Caravaggio. (p72)

**Museo Poldi Pezzoli**
Renaissance treasures displayed in artful historically
styled rooms. (p50)

**Museo Bagatti Valsecchi**
The Bagatti Valsecchi *palazzo*
(mansion) is a living mu-
seum of the Quattrocento.
(p53)

**Gallerie d'Italia** A vast
collection paying homage
to 18th- and 19th-century
Lombard painting. (p39)

## Best Modernists

**Galleria d'Arte Moderna**
Works from the 19th and
20th centuries feature in
Napoleon's neoclassical Villa
Reale. (p55)

**Museo del Novecento** Has
4000 sq metres designed
by Italo Rota to showcase

Italy's 20th-century talent.
(p36)

**Casa Museo Boschi-di
Stefano** Find 20th-century
greats crowded salon-style
in a Piero Portaluppi–
designed apartment. (p55)

## Best
Contemporary
Galleries

**Fondazione Prada** Miuccia Prada's mind-bending
contemporary art collection
is housed in a former brandy
factory. (p127)

**Museo delle Culture** This
David Chipperfield gallery
showcases exciting exhibits
focused on Milan's dialogue
with the wider world.
(pictured above; p115)

# Architecture

VIACHESLAV LOPATIN/SHUTTERSTOCK ©

*Milan's architectural charm lies in its mix of styles, but at the fore is the city's love affair with art nouveau and modernist architecture. Streets are lined with fin de siècle Liberty apartments that merge with 1930s rationalist rigour. What's more, the city leads the way with the biggest post-war development in Italy at Porta Nuova.*

## Best Period Architecture

**Duomo** Cloud-piercing Gothic spires in pink Candoglian marble. (p32)

**Castello Sforzesco** Monumental medieval architecture fashioned for a dynastic powerhouse. (p70)

**Basilica di Sant'Ambrogio** This much-rebuilt 4th-century church is a textbook example of local Lombard Romanesque style. (p103)

**Basilica di Santa Maria delle Grazie** This Bramante-domed basilica is a Unesco World Heritage Site. (p103)

**Chiesa di Santa Maria dei Miracoli e San Celso** Milan's only Renaissance church. (p127)

## Best Modern Architecture

**Galleria Vittorio Emanuele II** Europe's first shopping mall in an elegant art nouveau building. (p44)

**Villa Necchi Campiglio** Piero Portaluppi's exquisitely detailed rationalist home for two Milanese heiresses. (p55)

**Stazione Centrale** Milan's vast central station epitomises the muscular architecture favoured by Mussolini. (pictured above; p148)

**Torre Pirelli** Gio Ponti's Milanese landmark is one of Italy's earliest skyscrapers. (p55)

**Torre Velasca** Studio BBPR's utterly original 1950s fortress-apartment block inspired by medieval watchtowers. (p127)

## Best Contemporary Architecture

**Fondazione Prada** A Rem Koolhaas–designed gallery sets in a defunct brandy factory. (p127)

**Fondazione Feltrinelli** Herzog & de Meuron's eye-catching slanted glass structure is inspired by Milanese greenhouses. (p89)

**Museo delle Culture** David Chipperfield's translucent glass and concrete museum in a renovated electricity station. (p115)

# History

*The Romans didn't consider Cisalpine Gaul part of Italy at all. In 222 BC when they conquered the city of the Insubri Celts they named it Mediolanum (Middle of the Plains). Since then Milan has been home to imperial courts, supplied arms for various empires and flourished on the back of clever politicking, manufacturing and farming.*

BLUE PLANET STUDIO/SHUTTERSTOCK ©

## Best Roman Remains

**Civico Museo Archeologico** Home to Roman, Greek and Etruscan artefacts and a model of Roman Milan. (p104)

**Basilica di San Lorenzo** This early-Christian basilica retains its circular form and 16 Roman columns outside. (p115)

## Best of Medieval Milan

**Duomo** Crafted over 600 years, Milan's cathedral is one of the finest examples of Gothic architecture in the world. (p32)

**Castello Sforzesco** Milan's mighty medieval fortress is the repository of artworks

that tell the city's history. (pictured above; p70)

**Biblioteca e Pinacoteca Ambrosiana** Home to Leonardo da Vinci's priceless sketchbook, the *Codex Atlanticus*. (p39)

**Basilica di Sant'Ambrogio** Milan's spiritual home is filled with medieval masterpieces. (p103)

## Best of Renaissance Milan

**The Last Supper** Leonardo da Vinci's peerless mural depicting Christ at the moment he reveals his betrayal. (p98)

**Chiesa di Santa Maria Presso di San Satiro** Bramante's trick of false

perspective turns a tiny chapel into a full-sized church. (p40)

**Chiesa di San Maurizio** Filled with frescoes by da Vinci's contemporary Bernardino Luini. (p103)

## Best of 19th-Century Milan

**Palazzo Reale** This neoclassical palace is now a world-class museum. (p39)

**Cimitero Monumental** The final resting place of Milan's *haute bourgeoisie* with epic mausoleums. (p89)

**Galleria Vittorio Emanuele II** Milan's first shopping mall is adorned with mosaics and coloured marbles. (p44)

# Design

*Milan today is home to all the major design showrooms, the site of an endless round of influential international design fairs, and continues to be a centre of design education and publishing. Design here isn't merely functional, it is suffused with emotion – expressive, inventive, humorous and original.*

GIANLUCA DI IOIA- COURTESY: TRIENNALE DI MILANO. ©

## Who's Who

A visit to the Triennale di Milano design museum is a wonderful way to pay homage to the work of Italy's best and brightest designers. Many of these called, or continue to call, Milan home. Names to watch for include Gio Ponti, Bruno Munari, Piero Fornasetti, Enzo Mari, the Castiglioni brothers, Gaetano Pesce, Mario Bellini, Gae Aulenti, Ettore Sottsass and Alessandro Mendini.

## Best Design Inspiration

**Triennale di Milano** Museum, educational facility and showroom, the Triennale has championed design since the 1930s. (pictured above; p77)

**Studio Museo Achille Castiglioni** Tour the studio of one of Italy's most influential 20th-century designers. (p78)

**Villa Necchi Campiglio** Designed and decorated by modernist architect-designer Piero Portaluppi, this house is the definition of stylish living. (p55)

## Best Design Shops

**La Rinascente** The lower ground floor of this heritage department store is the launch pad for dozens of up-and-coming designers. (p45)

**Spazio Rossana Orlandi** An iconic interior design 'space' with out-of-the-ordinary objects and homewares. (p108)

**Alessi** All your favourite homewares are housed in this flagship store. (p53)

**Wok** Showcases avant-garde and emerging street labels, and hosts design and fashion events. (p120)

**43 Cycles** The most beautiful bikes in the world with cutting-edge engineering. (p62)

# Under the Radar Milan

*Beyond Milan's fashion boutiques, internationally acclaimed exhibitions and design fairs is the city's quieter side. Cycle and walk along miles of tree-lined canals, play ping pong with locals in offbeat piazzas and discover a vibrant contemporary cultural scene in the city's wealth of small bars, restaurants, galleries and cultural hubs.*

KEVIN FAINGNAERT/LONELY PLANET ©

## Cruise Milan's Canals

Milan, like Venice, was once networked with canals. Most of them were paved over with roads in the 20th century, but four remain – Naviglio Grande, Naviglio Martesana, Naviglio di Bereguardo and Canale Muzza – and offer great cycling and walking trails deep into the countryside.

## Offbeat Neighbourhoods

Milan is a city of distinct urban villages. Their individualism lends the city much of its energy. Explore charismatic Ortica (famous for its street art), multi-ethnic NoLo and nightlife locus Isola.

## Popular Local Pastimes

When summer temperatures sizzle, the Milanese head to the city's retro lidos such as Bagni Misteriosi, Piscina Giulio Romano and Centro Balneare Argelati.

In the past, Milan had dozens of dancehalls that catered to clocked-off workers, providing them with dinner and a place to do the *liscio* (northern Italian dance). La Balera dell-Ortica is one of the most popular, offering hearty food, bocce and lively swing and lindy hop nights.

Happy hour elsewhere might mean downing cut-price pints, but not in Milan. Here, the nightly *aperitivo* is a two- to three-hour ritual, including a drink and an unlimited buffet of delicious snacks. Don't miss out.

# Four Perfect Days

## Day 1

Rise early and climb to the roof of the **Duomo** (p32) for a bird's-eye view of the city. Break for a *spritz* at **Camparino** (p42), then head into the **Museo del Novecento** (p36) for some 20th-century art.

Sample top-notch Milanese dishes at **Trattoria Milanese** (p42) before moving on to **Castello Sforzesco** (p70) to explore Milan's history. Then change gears at the **Triennale** (p77), which is devoted to design.

Wander across Parco Sempione to watch the sunset on the **Arco della Pace** (pictured above; p77) from one of the bars that ring its base. Finally, catch tram 10 to Navigli and bar hop along the canal to the **Apollo Club** (p113).

## Day 2

Devote a whole morning to the masterpiece-packed halls of the **Pinacoteca di Brera** (pictured above; p72). You'll be rewarded with a stunning collection of works by Bellini, Raphael and Caravaggio. Then wander through Brera's chic, cobbled lanes.

Grab a gourmet sandwich at **De Santis** (p105) for lunch. Then ponder Bernardino Luini's tortured saints in the frescoes at **Chiesa di San Maurizio** (p103). Families will want to head to the **Museo Nazionale Scienza e Tecnologia** (p100), Italy's finest science museum.

Then, with prebooked tickets tour Leonardo da Vinci's **The Last Supper** (p98). Finish the night with dinner at **La Brisa** (p106), and drinks on the rooftop at **Ceresio 7** (p93).

## Day 3

MARIA ROM/SHUTTERSTOCK ©

Make a pilgrimage to **Gattullo** (p113) for decadent pastries. Then proceed to **Fondazione Prada** (pictured above; p127) for mind-bending contemporary art in the OMA-designed ex-brandy factory.

Lunch on homemade pasta at **Pastamadre** (p130), then continue to the Quadrilatero d'Oro. Have coffee at **Pasticceria Cova** (p53), and wander the high-fashion lanes buying small treats from **Sermoneta** (p65) and **Pellini** (p63).

End up at the **Museo Poldi Pezzoli** (p50), a one-time aristocratic home hung with priceless Renaissance artworks. Finish the night with cocktails at the **Spirit** (p131), dinner at **Trattoria del Pescatore** (p128) or live music at **Santeria Social Club** (p132).

## Day 4

YURI TURKOV/SHUTTERSTOCK ©

Choose one of Milan's lesser known museums for the morning: the avant-garde modern art collection at the **Boschi-di Stefano apartment** (p55) or the modernist house-museum **Villa Necchi Campiglio** (p55).

Then head to the fabulous Eataly food emporium for lunch at **Alice Ristorante** (p92). Afterwards, browse the shops along Corso Como and admire the skyscrapers of Porta Nuova. Then move on to the outdoor sculpture park that is the **Cimitero Monumentale** (pictured above; p89).

Sample some of the city's best wines and *aperitivo* (pre-dinner drinks) at **Cantine Isola** (p92) and then head to Isola to explore Milan's latest dining hot spots: **Casa Ramen Super** (p89) and **Berberè** (p90).

# Need to Know

For detailed information, see Survival Guide (p145)

**Language**
Italian

**Currency**
Euro (€)

**Visas**
Generally not required for stays of up to three months.

**Money**
ATMs are widely available and credit cards are universally accepted.

**Mobile Phones**
Italy uses GSM 900/1800, which is compatible with the rest of Europe and Australia.

**Time**
Central European Time (GMT/UTC plus one hour)

**Tipping**
**Top-end hotel** €2, for porter, maid or room service.
**Restaurant** 10-15% if service not included.
**Bar** €0.10 to €0.20 is fine.
**Taxi** Round up to the nearest euro.

## Daily Budget

### Budget: Less than €110
Dorm bed: €28–45
Gourmet sandwich: €5–12
*Aperitivo* cocktail & all-you-can-eat buffet: €8–20
Bus & metro ticket: €1.50

### Midrange: €110–200
Double room in a hotel: €120–200
Two-course lunch plus wine in local trattorias: €25–45
Museum admission: €5–10
Short taxi trip: €10

### Top End: More than €200
Double room in a four- or five-star hotel: €200–800
Dinner in a top restaurant: €50–150
Good seats at Teatro alla Scala opera house: €85–210

## Advance Planning

**Three months** Book accommodation if travelling during trade fairs, particularly during the Furniture Fair (April) and Fashion Weeks.

**Two months** Buy tickets for *The Last Supper* and Serie A football matches.

**One month** Reserve seats at La Scala, Michelin-starred restaurants and big shows at Palazzo Reale and MUDEC.

**One week** Check out *aperitivo* (pre-dinner drinks) hot spots and events at Zero (http://zero.eu/milano).

# Arriving in Milan

## ✈ From Milan Malpensa

Malpensa Express (📞 02 7249 4949; www.malpensaexpress.it; one-way €13) trains run between 5.50am and 12.20am; the Malpensa Shuttle (📞 02 5858 3185; www.malpensashuttle.it; one-way/return €8/14; Ⓜ Centrale) bus runs between 12.20am and 5.50am. Taxis are €90 (50 mins).

## ✈ From Milan Linate

Airport Bus Express (📞 02 3391 0794; www.airportbusexpress.it; one way/return €5/9; Ⓜ Centrale) runs to Stazione Centrale between 5.30am and 10pm; Air Bus (www.atm-mi.it; Piazza Luigi Savoia; adult/child €5/2.50; Ⓜ Centrale) offers a similar service. City bus 73 departs to Via Gonzaga (€1.50) every 10 to 20 minutes between 5.35am and 12.35am. Taxis cost €20 to €30.

# Getting Around

## Ⓜ Metro

The quickest way to get around. Runs roughly 5.40am to 12.20am (from 6.15am on Sunday).

## 🚋 Tram

Best for reaching areas in the south and northwest of the city; also good for sightseeing.

## 🚕 Taxi

Taxis must be picked up at designated ranks. Call a cab on 📞 02 40 40, 📞 02 69 69 or 📞 02 85 85. The meter runs from receipt of call.

## 🚲 Bike

Floating bikes and cycle lanes make this an option for the historic centre.

# Milan Neighbourhoods

**Porta Garibaldi & Isola (p85)**
Porta Nuova's shiny skyscrapers and buzzing Corso Garibaldi are showpieces for modern Milan. In their shadow up-and-coming Isola has a cool, multicultural vibe.

**Brera & Parco Sempione (p69)**
Brera's cute shops, art galleries and boho raffishness contrast with the grandeur of Castello Sforzesco and the Triennale design museum.

**Corso Magenta & Sant'Ambrogio (p97)**
A warren of medieval streets surrounds the Basilica di Sant'Ambrogio, while Corso Magenta is lined by patrician palaces.

**Navigli (p111)**
The south of the city is bisected by canals and is where the hipster kids come to shop, drink and party.

*Pinacoteca di Brera*

*Castello Sforzesco*

*The Last Supper*

*Museo Nazionale Scienza e Tecnologia Leonardo da Vinci*

*Museo del Novecento*

## Quadrilatero d'Oro & Giardini Pubblici (p49)

Milan's luxury enclave contains cobbled streets filled with high-fashion theatre, flanked by a pretty pleasure garden.

## Duomo & San Babila (p31)

Milan's historic hub is dominated by the twin temples of the Duomo and the Galleria Vittorio Emanuele II.

*Museo Poldi Pezzoli*

⊙ *Duomo*

## Porta Romana & Porta Vittoria (p125)

Miuccia Prada's fabulous Fondazione Prada is pioneering the revitalisation of this quiet corner of the city.

# Explore
# Milan

Galleria Vittorio Emanuele II (p44) BORIS STROUJKO/SHUTTERSTOCK ©

# Explore ⊙

# Duomo & San Babila

*Milan's centre is conveniently compact. The splendid cathedral sits in a vast piazza which throngs with tourists, touts and the Milanese themselves. From here, choose God or Mammon, art or music, or take in all four in the historic shopping arcade Galleria Vittorio Emanuele II (p44), La Scala opera house (p43) and the museums of the Palazzo Reale (p39) and Gallerie d'Italia (p39).*

*Any trip to Milan should start with a pilgrimage to the Duomo (p32) for a stroll among the saints adorning the parapets. You may even be able to spy the Alps over the evolving cityscape. Break for a mid-morning spritz (cocktail with prosecco) at Camparino (p42) and then check out the latest exhibition at the Palazzo Reale. For lunch, try traditional dishes at Trattoria da Pino (p41), before visiting Milan's modernist showcase, the Museo del Novecento (p36). It will then be time to join shoppers in the Galleria Vittorio Emanuele II. Opera and ballet fans will need to plan well ahead for a night at La Scala.*

## Getting There & Around

Ⓜ Take the east–west red line (M1) for Duomo, which brings you out in front of the cathedral. The north–south yellow line (M3) also connects here from the Stazione Centrale.

🚋 Numerous trams stop at Piazza del Duomo; the most useful are trams 1, 2, 3, 15 and 9.

### Duomo & San Babila Map on p38

Duomo (p32) KAVALENKAVA/SHUTTERSTOCK ©

## Top Experience 📷
# Climb to the Roof of the Duomo

*A vision in pink Candoglia marble, Milan's cath-edral reflects the city's creative brio and ambition. Begun by Giangaleazzo Visconti in 1387, its design was considered unfeasible. Canals had to be dug to transport the marble to the city centre, and new technologies were invented to deal with its enormous scale. Now its white facade rises like the filigree of a fairy-tale tiara and wows the crowds with its extravagant details.*

◉ MAP P38, D3

www.duomomilano.it

Piazza del Duomo

adult/reduced Duomo €3/2, roof terraces via stairs €9/4.50, lift €13/7, archaeological area €7/3

🕑 9am-7pm

Ⓜ Duomo

## The Exterior

During his stint as king of Italy, Napoleon offered to fund the Duomo's completion in 1805, in time for his coronation. The architect piled on the neo-Gothic details, a homage to the original design that displayed a prescient use of fashion logic – ie everything old is new again. The petrified pinnacles, cusps, buttresses, arches and more than 3000 statues are almost all products of the 19th century.

## Roof Terraces & Lantern

Climb to the roof terraces, where you'll be within touching distance of the elaborate 135 spires and their forest of flying buttresses. In the centre of the roof rises the 15th-century octagonal lantern and spire, on top of which is the golden Madonnina (erected in 1774). For centuries she was the highest point in the city (108.5m), until the Pirelli skyscraper outdid her in 1958.

## The Interior

Initially designed to accommodate Milan's then population of around 40,000, the cathedral's elegant, hysterical and sublimely spiritual architecture can transport 21st-century types back to a medieval mindset. Once your eyes have adjusted to the subdued light and surreal proportions inside (there are five grandiose naves supported by 52 columns), stare up, and up, to the largest stained-glass windows in Christendom.

## The Floors

Before you wander among the cathedral's many treasures, look down and marvel at the polychrome marble floor that sweeps across 12,000 sq metres. The design was conceived by Pellegrino Tibaldi and took 400 years to complete. The pink and white blocks

### ★ Top Tips

o Hours for the treasury, crypt, baptistry and roof vary, so check the website.

o The €16 combination ticket for the roof terraces, baptistry and treasury is a good deal, and it's valid for 72 hours.

o It's quicker to ascend to the roof via the 165 steps rather than using the tiny elevator.

o Purchase tickets online (www.duomo milano.it) for an extra €0.50 charge.

o Pre-bought tickets do not allow you to skip security checks.

### ✗ Take a Break

Nip into Iginio Massari (p41) for award-winning cream puffs.

Lunch at Trattoria Milanese (p42).

of Candoglia marble came from the cathedral's own quarries at Mergozzo (bequeathed in perpetuity by Giangaleazzo), and are inlaid with black marble from Varenna and red marble from Arzo.

## The Sundial

On the floor by the main entrance you may notice a brass strip lined with signs of the zodiac. This is, in fact, an 18th-century sundial, installed by astronomers from the Accademia di Brera in 1768. A hole in the vault of the south aisle casts a ray of sunlight at various points along its length (depending on the season) at astronomical noon. The device was so precise that all the city's clocks were set by it up until the 19th century.

## St Bartholomew

One of the cathedral's more unusual statues is the 1562 figure of St Bartholomew by Marco d'Agrate, a student of Leonardo da Vinci. It depicts St Bartholomew post-torture with his skin flayed from his flesh and cast about his neck like a cape. He was a favourite subject for 16th-century sculptors, enabling them to show off their anatomical knowledge as well as their technique.

## The Transept

Bisecting the nave, the transept is especially rich in works of art. At either end there is an altar decorated with polychrome marbles, the most elaborate being the *Altar to the Virgin of the Tree* on the north side.

## Milan Duomo

In front of this stands the monumental, 5m-high Trivulzio candelabrum, a masterpiece of medieval bronze work, its seven branches inset with precious stones.

## The Choir

Completed in 1614, the sculpted choir stalls were designed by Pellegrino Tibaldi and carved by Paolo de'Gazzi, Virgilio del Conte and the Taurini brothers. The three tiers of sculpture represent the life of Milanese bishops Anatalone and Galdino at the base, the martyred saints in the centre and the life of St Ambrose above.

## The Crypt

From the ambulatory that encircles the choir are the stairs down to the crypt or Winter Choir. Designed by Tibaldi, this jewel-like circular chapel with its red porphyry pillars, polychrome marble floor and stucco ceiling contains a casket holding the relics of various saints and martyrs. A wooden choir stall encircles the room.

## Scurolo di San Carlo

Through a gap in the crypt's choir stalls, a dark corridor leads to a memorial chapel housing the remains of saintly Carlo Borromeo (cardinal archbishop of Milan; 1564–84), contained in a rock-crystal casket atop a silver altar.

### Adopt a Spire

With 3400 marble statues, 200 bas-reliefs, 55 stained-glass windows, 96 gargoyles and an internal area of 11,700-sq-metres, the job of maintaining the cathedral is an awesome responsibility. In 2012, the Veneranda launched a major new fund-raising campaign that has seen to the cleaning and repair of many aspects of this beautiful monument. You, too, can chip in by joining the Adopt a Spire (www.getyourspire.com) campaign, where for as little as €10 you can choose a spire and even have your name engraved on it for posterity.

## Il Grande Museo del Duomo

Included in the ticket to the Duomo is entrance to the cathedral's stunning **museum** (Piazza del Duomo 12; ⏱10am-6pm Thu-Tue). Designed by Guido Canali, its glowing spaces look like sets for an episode of *Game of Thrones*. Gargoyles leer down through the shadows; shafts of light strike the wings of heraldic angels; and a monstrous godhead, once intended for the high altar, glitters awesomely in copper. It's an exciting display, masterfully choreographed through 26 rooms, which tell the 600-year story of the cathedral's construction.

## Top Experience 📷
# Get Arty at Museo del Novecento

*Overlooking Piazza del Duomo, with fabulous views of the cathedral, Mussolini's Palazzo dell'Arengario is where he would harangue huge crowds in the glory days of his regime. It's now home to Milan's museum of 20th-century art. Built around a futuristic spiral ramp (an ode to the Guggenheim), the heady collection includes the likes of Boccioni, Campigli, Giorgio de Chirico and Marinetti.*

◉ MAP P38, C3

www.museodelnovecento.org

Via Marconi 1

adult/reduced €10/8

🕐 2.30-7.30pm Mon, from 9.30am Tue, Wed, Fri & Sun, to 10.30pm Thu & Sat

Ⓜ Duomo

## Palazzo dell'Arengario

The austere Arengario consists of two symmetrical buildings each with a three-tier arcaded facade.

It was built in the 1950s by star architects Piero Portaluppi, Giovanni Muzio, Pier Giulio Magistretti and Enrico Griffini, and is decorated with bas-reliefs by Milanese sculptor Arturo Martini, whose work now features in the museum's collection.

The name *arengario* comes from the building's original function as the government seat during the Fascist period, when officials would *arringa* (harangue) the local populous from the building's balcony.

## The Collection

The museum's permanent collection is an ode to 20th-century modern art, and has a particular focus on Milanese home-grown talent.

Chronological rooms take you from Volpedo's powerful neo-Impressionist painting of striking workers, *Il quarto stato* (*The Fourth Estate;* 1901), through the dynamic work of futurist greats such as Umberto Boccioni, Carlo Carra, Gino Severini and Giacomo Balla, then on to abstractism, surrealism, spatialism and Arte Povera.

The collection provides a fascinating social commentary on Italy's trajectory through two world wars and into the technological era.

★ **Top Tips**

o Audioguides are available in English, Italian, French, German and Spanish.

o The museum is accessible with the official Tourist MuseumCard, which costs €12 and gives access to nine other civic museums.

o There's a reduced admission price of €6 every Tuesday from 2pm and every day two hours before closing.

o Some of the best views of the Duomo are to be had on Level 3, standing beneath Lucio Fontana's fluorescent light: *Luce spaziale: struttura al neon* (1951).

✘ **Take a Break**

In the evening, find your way down the historic back streets to hip B Cafè (p43) for cocktails.

**Duomo & San Babila** Get Arty at Museo del Novecento

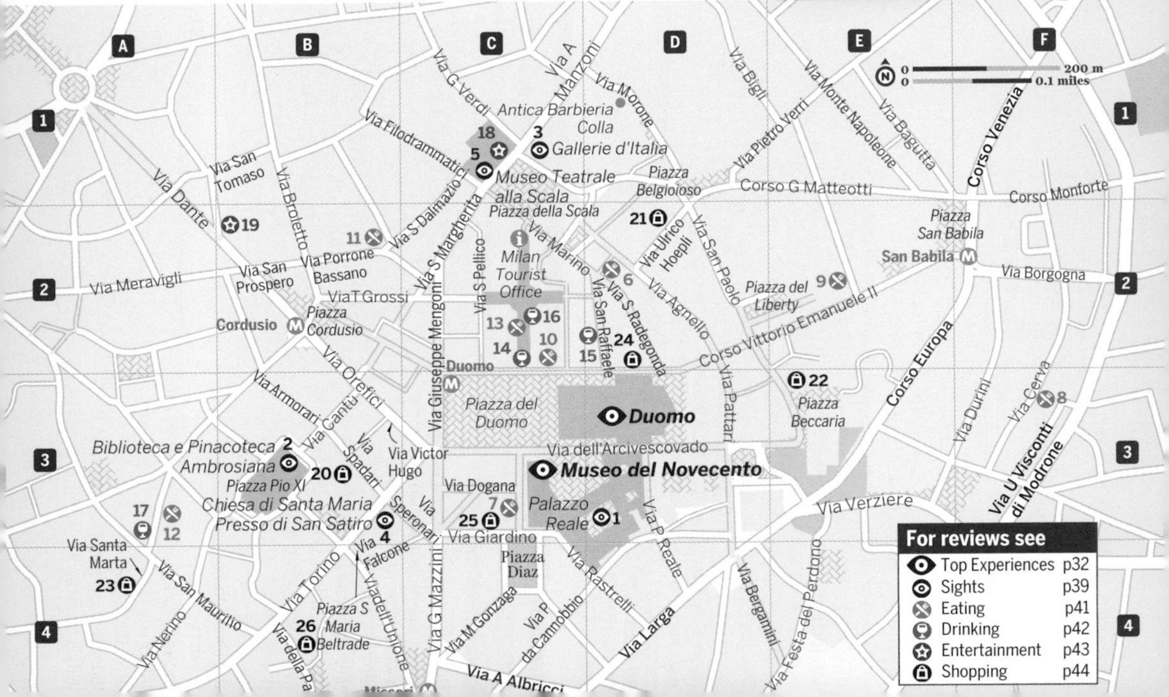
A
B
C
D
E
F
1
2
3
4
200 m
0.1 miles
Via A Manzoni
Via G Verdi
Antica Barbieria Colla
Via Morone
18
5
3
Gallerie d'Italia
Via Filodrammatici
Museo Teatrale alla Scala
Piazza della Scala
Via San Tomaso
Via Dante
19
Via Broletto
Via S Dalmazio
Via S Margherita
Via S Pellico
11
Via Porrone Bassano
Via San Prospero
Via Meravigli
Via T Grossi
Piazza Cordusio
Cordusio
Milan Tourist Office
Via Marino
13
16
14
10
15
24
6
Via San Raffaele
Via S Radegonda
Via Agnello
Via Ulrico Hoepli
Via San Paolo
Piazza Belgioioso
21
Corso G Matteotti
Via Pietro Verri
Via Bigli
Via Monte Napoleone
Via Bagutta
Corso Venezia
Corso Monforte
Piazza San Babila
San Babila
Via Borgogna
Piazza del Liberty
9
Corso Vittorio Emanuele II
Corso Europa
22
Piazza Beccaria
Via Durini
Via Cerva
8
Via U Visconti di Modrone
Via Orefici
Via Giuseppe Mengoni
Duomo
Piazza del Duomo
Duomo
Via Pattari
Via dell'Arcivescovado
Museo del Novecento
Via Armorari
Via Cantù
Via Spadari
Via Victor Hugo
Biblioteca e Pinacoteca Ambrosiana
2
20
Piazza Pio XI
Chiesa di Santa Maria Presso di San Satiro
Via Speronari
4
Via Falcone
Via Dogana
7
25
Via Giardino
Palazzo Reale
1
Piazza Diaz
Via P Reale
Via Rastrelli
Via Verziere
17
12
Via Santa Marta
23
Via San Maurilio
Via Nerino
Via Torino
Piazza S Maria Beltrade
26
Via della Pa
Viadell'Unione
Via G Mazzini
Via M Gonzaga
Via P da Cannobbio
Via Larga
Via Bergamini
Via Festa del Perdono
Via A Albricci
For reviews see
Top Experiences p32
Sights p39
Eating p41
Drinking p42
Entertainment p43
Shopping p44

# Sights

## Palazzo Reale

MUSEUM, PALACE

**1** ◉ MAP P38, D3

Empress Maria Theresa's favourite architect, Giuseppe Piermarini, gave this town hall and Visconti palace a neoclassical overhaul in the late 18th century. The supremely elegant interiors were all but destroyed by WWII bombs; the **Sala delle Cariatidi** remains unrenovated as a reminder of war's destruction. Now the once opulent palace hosts blockbuster art exhibits, attracting serious crowds to shows featuring artists as diverse as Escher, Caravaggio and Pomodoro. (www. palazzorealemilano.it; Piazza del Duomo 12; admission varies; ⏲2.30-7.30pm Mon, from 9.30am Tue, Wed, Fri & Sun, to 10.30pm Thu & Sat; Ⓜ Duomo)

## Biblioteca e Pinacoteca Ambrosiana

GALLERY, LIBRARY

**2** ◉ MAP P38, B3

Europe's first public library, built in 1609, the Biblioteca Ambrosiana was more a symbol of intellectual ferment than of quiet scholarship. It houses more than 75,000 volumes and 35,000 manuscripts including Leonardo da Vinci's priceless collection of drawings, the *Codex Atlantic*. An art gallery – the Pinacoteca – was added later. It exhibits Italian paintings from the 14th to the 20th century, most famously Caravaggio's *Canestra di frutta (Basket of Fruit)*, which launched both his career and Italy's ultrarealist traditions. (www. ambrosiana.it; Piazza Pio XI 2; adult/ reduced €15/10; ⏲10am-6pm Tue-Sun; Ⓜ Duomo)

## Gallerie d'Italia

MUSEUM

**3** ◉ MAP P38, C1

Housed in three fabulously decorated palaces, the enormous art collection of Fondazione Cariplo and Intesa Sanpaolo bank pays homage to 18th- and 19th-century Lombard painting. From a magnificent sequence of bas-reliefs by Antonio Canova to luminous Romantic masterpieces by Francesco Hayez, the works span 23 rooms and document Milan's significant contribution to the rebirth of Italian sculpture, the patriotic romanticism of the Risorgimento (reunification period) and the birth of futurism at the dawn of the 20th century. (www.gallerieditalia.com; Piazza della Scala 6; adult/reduced

### Antica Barbieria Colla

Take a pew next to politicians, football stars and businessmen and let jovial Franco Bompieri steam, lather and close shave you into a state of bliss. Opened in 1904, **Antica Barbieria Colla** (Map p38, D1; ☏02 87 43 12; www.anticabarbieriacolla.it; Via Morone 3; ⏲8.30am-12.30pm & 2.30-7pm Tue-Sun; Ⓜ Duomo, 🚋1) is the oldest barber shop in Europe and was once frequented by Puccini, whose shaving brush is proudly displayed.

€10/8; ⊙9.30am-7.30pm Tue-Wed & Fri-Sun, to 10.30pm Thu; M Duomo)

## Chiesa di Santa Maria Presso di San Satiro  CHURCH

4 ⊙ MAP P38, B3

Here's an escape from the Zara/Benetton/H&M maelstrom on Via Torino. Ludovico Sforza saw potential in this little church built on top of the 9th-century mausoleum of martyr San Satiro, and asked architect Donato Bramante to refurbish it in 1482. His ambition wasn't dampened by the project's scale: a *trompe l'œil*–coffered niche on the shallow apse makes the backdrop to the altar mimic the Pantheon in Rome. (Via Torino 17; admission free; ⊙9.30am-5.30pm Tue-Sat, 2-5.30pm Sun; M Duomo)

## Museo Teatrale alla Scala  MUSEUM

5 ⊙ MAP P38, C1

Giuseppe Piermarini's 2800-seat theatre was inaugurated in 1778, replacing the previous theatre, which burnt down in a fire after a carnival gala. Costs were covered by the sale of *palchi* (private boxes), of which there are six gilt-and-crimson tiers. Outside rehearsals you can stand in boxes 13, 15 and 18 for a glimpse of the interior, while in the museum harlequin costumes and a spinet inscribed with the command 'Inexpert hand, touch me not!' hint at centuries of musical drama. (La Scala Museum; www.museoscala.org; Largo Ghiringhelli 1; adult/reduced €9/6; ⊙9am-5.30pm; M Duomo)

Biblioteca e Pinacoteca Ambrosiana (p39)

# Eating

### Luini
FAST FOOD $

6 ⊗ MAP P38, D2

This historic joint is the go-to place for *panzerotti,* delicious pizza-dough parcels stuffed with a combination of mozzarella, spinach, tomato, ham or spicy salami, and then fried or baked in a wood-fired oven. (☎02 8646 1917; www.luini.it; Via Santa Radegonda 16; panzerotti €2.70; ⊙10am-3pm Mon, to 8pm Tue-Sat; ♿; Ⓜ Duomo)

### Iginio Massari
PASTRIES $

7 ⊗ MAP P38, C3

Iginio Massari has topped pretty much every pastry guide, is a winner of Venice's Golden Lion for Lifetime Achievement and is a master of northern Italy's two signature desserts: Verona's *pandoro* and Milan's *panettone.* Crowds mobbed the opening of his new Milanese *pasticceria* in 2018 to secure one of his famous *bignes* (cream puffs) filled with Chantilly cream and chocolate. (☎02 4969 6962; www.iginiomassari.it; Via Marconi 4; pastries & cake slices €1.50-6; ⊙7.30am-8pm Mon-Fri, from 8.30am Sat & Sun; ❄; Ⓜ Duomo)

### Trattoria da Pino
MILANESE $

8 ⊗ MAP P38, F3

In a city full of models in Michelin-starred restaurants, working-class da Pino offers the perfect antidote. Sit elbow-to-elbow at long cafeteria-style tables and order up bowls of *bollito misto* (mixed boiled meats), handmade pasta and curried veal nuggets. (☎02 7600 0532 Via Cerva 14; meals €20-25; ⊙noon-3pm Mon-Sat; Ⓜ San Babila)

### A Santa Lucia
NEAPOLITAN $$

9 ⊗ MAP P38, E2

Part of one of the great waves of migration from the south, Leone and Rosetta Legnani opened their first restaurant in 1929. They brought with them their warm-hearted Neapolitan cooking and old-school southern style, with plates of *spaghetti alla vongole* (spaghetti with clams) and garlic-slathered steaks delivered by waiters wearing impeccable white jackets. No wonder Frank Sinatra liked this place. (☎02 7602 3155; www.asantalucia.it; Via San Pietro all'Orto 3; meals €25-50; ⊙noon-1am; Ⓜ San Babila)

### Spazio
ITALIAN $$

10 ⊗ MAP P38, C2

Located on the fourth floor of the Mercato del Duomo is chef Niko Romito's low-key restaurant run by graduates of his culinary school in Abruzzo (where you'll find his three-Michelin-starred restaurant). Reserve a seat in the Sala dell'Albero and you'll get an eyeful of the Duomo alongside delightfully unfussy plates of lemon pasta, and linguine with broccoli rabe and anchovies. (4th fl, Mercato del Duomo; ☎06 8535 2523; www.spazionikoromito.com; Piazza del Duomo; meals €35-45; ⊙12.30-2.30pm & 7.30-10pm; ❄; Ⓜ Duomo)

## T'a Milano
MILANESE $$

11 MAP P38, B2

Chocolatiers Tancredi and Alberto Alemagna's Milanese outlet is a beautiful space. Aside from the counters crammed with delectable chocolates, the dining room is a delight to behold: huge marble floor tiles, sapphire-blue banquettes and glowing 1950s brass lamps. The chic crowd of diners come for king crab sandwiches, fillet of San Pietro fish and, of course, the chocolate Duomo cake. (www.tamilano.com; Via Clerici 1; meals €25-45; 8am-3pm & 6pm-midnight Tue-Sat, to 9.30pm Mon; M Cordusio)

## Trattoria Milanese
MILANESE $$

12 MAP P38, A3

Like an old friend you haven't seen in years, this trattoria welcomes you with generous goblets of wine, hearty servings of traditional Milanese fare and convivial banter over the vegetable buffet. Regulars slide into their seats, barely needing to order as waiters bring them their usual: meatballs wrapped in cabbage, minestrone or the sinfully good *risotto al salto* (refried risotto). (02 8645 1991; Via Santa Marta 11; meals €35-45; noon-3pm & 7-11.30pm Mon-Fri; 2, 14)

## Cracco
ITALIAN $$$

13 MAP P38, C2

Following a tumble from grace and a lost Michelin star, Carlo Cracco is back with a four-storey food temple in the Galleria. You can nibble brioche by Luca Sacchi, pralines from Marco Pedron, and overpriced pizza in the bistro, but the star remains the gourmet restaurant with its inventive haute cuisine including red snapper with yuzu jelly and shaved scallops. (www.ristorantecracco.it; Galleria Vittorio Emanuele II; tasting menu €190, bistro meals €30-50; 8am-midnight; M Duomo)

# Drinking

## Camparino in Galleria
BAR

14 MAP P38, C2

Open since the inauguration of the Galleria Vittorio Emanuele II arcade in 1867, this art nouveau bar has served drinks to the likes of Verdi, Toscanini and Dudovich. Cast-iron chandeliers and huge mirrored walls trimmed with mosaics of birds and flowers set the tone for a classy Campari-based cocktail. Drink at the bar for one of the cheapest *aperitivo* (pre-dinner drinks and snacks) in town. (www.camparino.it; Piazza del Duomo 21; drinks €12-24; 7.30am-8pm Tue-Sun; M Duomo)

## Straf Bar
BAR

15 MAP P38, D2

A nightly *aperitivo* scene kicks on until pumpkin hour at the Straf's super-sexy hotel bar. The decor is along the mod-exotic lines: wood, metal and stone played up against minimalist concrete. On Thursdays the bar hosts regular international DJs; on Tuesdays there is live music. (www.straf.it; Via San Raffaele 3; 11am-midnight; M Duomo)

## Pasticceria Marchesi CAFE

16 🚇 MAP P38, C2

With an 80% stake in the historic bakery, Prada has installed a luxurious cafe on the 1st floor of its menswear store in the Galleria. Overlooking the mosaics down below, the lounge is decked out in green floral jacquard and velvet armchairs. Come for high tea or the excellent *aperitivo*, although expect a wait as service is snooze-inducing. (www.pasticceriamarchesi.it; Galleria Vittorio Emanuele II; ⊙7.30am-9pm; M Duomo)

## B Cafè BAR

17 🚇 MAP P38, A3

Step into this cool cafe and you could be forgiven for thinking you'd landed in Brooklyn. Exposed brick walls and vintage movie posters give it a laid-back vibe, while the spirit-backed bar delivers well-crafted cocktails. It's a relaxed place for a coffee, glass of wine or a superior sandwich stuffed with cold cuts and Lombard cheeses throughout the day. (📞02 8909 3317; www.facebook.com/bcafe20; Via San Maurilio 20; sandwiches €5-6, cocktails €8; ⊙8am-1am Mon-Thu, to 2am Fri & Sat; 🛜; M Missori)

# Entertainment

## Teatro alla Scala OPERA

18 ⭐ MAP P38, C1

One of the most famous opera stages in the world, La Scala's season runs from early December to July. You can also see theatre, ballet and concerts here year-round (except August). Buy tickets online

Camparino in Galleria

or by phone up to two months before the performance, or from the central **box office** (Largo Ghiringhelli; noon-6pm; M Duomo). On performance days, tickets for the gallery are available from the box office at Via Filodrammatici 2 (one ticket per customer). Queue early. (La Scala; 02 7200 3744; www.teatroallascala.org; Piazza della Scala; tickets €30-300; M Duomo)

### Piccolo Teatro Grassi    THEATRE

19 ⭐ MAP P38, B2

This risk-taking little repertory theatre was opened in 1947 by Paolo Grassi and theatre director Giorgio Strehler, who then embarked on a nationwide movement of avant-garde productions and Commedia dell'Arte revivals. Additional programming, including ballet, goes on at sibling space, Teatro Strehler (p81). (02 4241 1889; www.piccoloteatro.org; Via Rovello 2; tickets €12-30; M Cordusio)

#### Galleria Vittorio Emanuele II

So much more than a shopping arcade, the neoclassical **Galleria Vittorio Emanuele II** (Piazza del Duomo; M Duomo) is a soaring iron-and-glass structure known locally as *il salottobueno*, the city's fine drawing room. Shaped like a crucifix, it also marks the *passeggiata* (evening stroll) route from Piazza del Duomo to Piazza di Marino and the doors of La Scala.

# Shopping

## Peck    FOOD & DRINKS

20 🔒 MAP P38, B3

Milan's historic deli is a bastion of the city's culinary heritage with three floors below ground dedicated to turning out the fabulously colourful display of foods that cram every counter. It showcases a mind-boggling selection of cheeses, chocolates, pralines, pastries, freshly made gelato, seafood, meat, caviar, pâté, fruit and vegetables, olive oils and balsamic vinegars. (02 802 31 61; www.peck.it; Via Spadari 9; 3-8pm Mon, from 9am Tue-Sat, 10am-5pm Sun; ; M Duomo)

### Libreria Internazionale Hoepli    BOOKS

21 🔒 MAP P38, D2

Italy's largest bookshop has six floors and some 500,000 titles plus rare antiquarian books, as well as English- and German-language sections. Don't neglect to browse the Italian shelves; local publishers are known for their beautiful cover design and innovative pictorial titles. (02 86 48 71; www.hoepli.it; Via Ulrico Hoepli 5; 10am-7.30pm Mon-Sat; ; M Duomo)

### Excelsior Milano    DEPARTMENT STORE

22 🔒 MAP P38, E3

Designed by star architect Jean Nouvel, this former cinema is a futuristic space halfway between a luxury department store and an innovative concept store. Six levels tantalise with everything from high-end fashion to gourmet foods, niche perfumes and tech gadgets. (☎02 7630 7301; www.excelsiormilano.com; Galleria del Corso 4; ⏰10am-8.30pm; Ⓜ San Babila)

## Wait and See    FASHION & ACCESSORIES

### 23 🅰 MAP P38, A4

With collaborations with international brands and designers such as Missoni, Etro and Anna Molinari under her belt, Uberta Zambeletti launched her own collection in 2010. Quirky Wait and See indulges her eclectic tastes and showcases unfamiliar brands alongside items exclusively designed for the store, including super-fun La Prestic Ouiston print tops and Meher Kakalia embroidered sandals. (☎02 7208 0195; www.waitandsee.it; Via Santa Marta 14; ⏰3.30-7.30pm Mon, from 10.30am Tue-Sat; Ⓜ Duomo, Missori)

## La Rinascente    DEPARTMENT STORE

### 24 🅰 MAP P38, D2

Italy's most prestigious department store doesn't let the fashion capital down – come for Italian diffusion lines, French lovelies and LA upstarts. The basement also hides a 'Made in Italy' design supermarket, and chic hairdresser Aldo Coppola is on the top floor. Take away edible souvenirs from the 7th-floor food market and dine out on Obikà's terrace with views of the Duomo. (☎02 8 85 21; www.rinascente.it; Piazza del Duomo; ⏰9.30am-9pm Mon-Thu & Sun, to 10pm Sat; Ⓜ Duomo)

## One Block Down    FASHION & ACCESSORIES

### 25 🅰 MAP P38, C3

This store is a temple for streetwear lovers started by a group of self-confessed sneaker freaks. A curated wall of sneakers goes all the way up to its high ceilings; there's clothing from Palace and Adidas, plus a selection of edgy magazines. If you're suffering from sneaker overload, take a quick break in the health food–focused in-store cafe, Flavours. (☎02 8454 2491; www.oneblockdown.it; Piazza Diaz 2; ⏰11am-8pm; Ⓜ Duomo)

## Federico Monzani    FASHION & ACCESSORIES

### 26 🅰 MAP P38, B4

You can't fail to notice illustrator Federico Monzani's joyful shop window sporting a host of his imaginative cartoon characters, graphic T-shirts and artworks. Favourites include bags printed with his Vitruvian Alien and tees sporting his 'Ettore' style multi-coloured chameleon and Rubik's cube. (☎02 8347 5465; www.shop.federicomonzani.com; Via della Palla 3; ⏰11.30am-2.30pm & 3.30-7.30pm Wed-Fri, from 10.30am Sat, 3.30-7.30pm Sun & Tue; Ⓜ Missori)

# Walking Tour 🥾

# Historic Milan

*Ruled by the Caesars, Napoleon and Mussolini, Milan's strategic position has made for a fascinating history. Mercantile Milan invented the idea of the city-state, and the Edict of Milan (313 CE) ended the persecution of Christians. From Roman origins to Republican ambitions and industrial pretensions, this walk takes you through Milan's most tumultuous events.*

## Walk Facts

**Start** Piazza del Duomo;
🚇 Duomo

**End** Piazza Castello;
🚇 Cairoli

**Length** 3.2km; 1½ hours

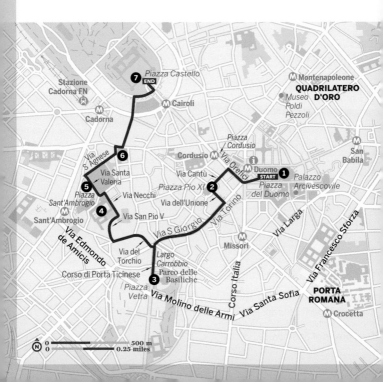

## ❶ The Duomo

Milan's pearly white Duomo (p32), covered in a panthcon of marble saints, is the third-largest cathedral in the world. A gift from Giangaleazzo Visconti, who started works in 1386, its centuries-long creation maps much of the history of Milan.

## ❷ Biblioteca Ambrosiana

Blazing an intellectual trail out of the Dark Ages, Cardinal Federico Borromeo founded one of Italy's greatest libraries, the Biblioteca Ambrosiana (p39), in 1609. Among its collection are pages from da Vinci's compendium of drawings, the *Codex Atlanticus*.

## ❸ San Lorenzo Columns

Roman Mediolanum once had its forum in Piazza Carrobbio. Nearby, the 16 Corinthian columns that now stand as portico to the Basilica di San Lorenzo (p115) were originally part of a Roman temple or bath. Nearby on Via Edmondo de Amicis are the ruins of the amphitheatre.

## ❹ Basilica di Sant'Ambrogio

Sant'Ambrogio (p103) was built on a paleo-Christian burial site and houses the bones of Milan's favourite bishop, St Ambrose. Its mongrel Lombard Romanesque style speaks volumes of history. The oldest part is the apse, featuring 4th-century mosaics depicting the *Miracle of St Ambrose*.

## ❺ Tempio della Vittoria

The **Temple of Victory** (Piazza Sant'Ambrogio; Ⓜ Sant'Ambrogio) commemorates 10,000 victims of the 'Great War', WWI. Designed by Giovanni Munzio, its unadorned appearance caused much controversy in depressed, postwar Milan.

## ❻ Civico Museo Archeologico

Foundation walls of Roman Milan and a medieval tower form part of Milan's Archaeological Museum (p104), which houses a model of the Roman city and precious remnants of glass, grave goods and jewellery.

## ❼ Castello Sforzesco

The Castello Sforzesco (p70), a turreted castle, embodies Milan's chameleon-like survival instincts. The art within it charts the rise and fall of the city's fortunes and many of its halls were frescoed by Leonardo da Vinci.

### ✕ Take a Break

Liberty-style **Bar Magenta** (☎ 02 805 38 08; www.bar magenta.it; Via Carducci 13; ⏱ 7.30am-2.30am Sun-Thu, to 4.30am Fri & Sat; Ⓜ Cadorna) on Corso Magenta is a good midpoint stop. Alternatively, plan to finish with an *aperitivo* (pre-dinner drink) at Bar Bianco (p71).

# Explore ◈

# Quadrilatero d'Oro & Giardini Pubblici

*The Quadrilatero d'Oro (Golden Quad) sings a siren song to luxury-label lovers the world over. This 6000-sq-metre area is home to over 500 of the world's top fashion brands interspersed with historic palace museums and heritage restaurants. To the northeast is the 19th-century public garden framed by the Villa Reale.*

*Start the day at Cova (p53), the Quad's most historic cafe. Then tour the art-filled apartment of the Museo Poldi Pezzoli (p50). You'll need to put on your shades as you trot between the two to avoid being dazzled by the Quad's display of luxury goods. Come lunchtime opt for Michelin-starred Mediterranean food in the cloister of La Veranda (p59) or a trip down memory lane at traditional Il Baretto (p58). Wander north to the Giardini Pubblici (p56) in the afternoon. Visit Napoleon's Villa Reale (p55), now Milan's museum of early 20th-century art; and then the offbeat apartment of the Casa Museo Boschi-di Stefano (p55), which is decked out with futurist art. Aperitivo then beckons at Bar Basso (p61) or LùBar (p58).*

## Getting There & Around

🚇 Take the M3 (yellow line) for the Quad and exit at Montenapoleone. For the south end of the Giardini and the Villa Reale take the M1 (red line) and exit at Palestro; for the north end of the garden exit at Porta Venezia. For the Museo Boschi-di Stefano, exit the M1 at Lima.

🚊 Trams 1, 9 and 33 are convenient for the Quad, Giardini and Porta Venezia.

## Quadrilatero d'Oro Map on p54

## Top Experience 📷
# Discover Renaissance Artworks at Museo Poldi Pezzoli

*Inheriting his fortune at the age of 24, Gian Giacomo Poldi Pezzoli also inherited his mother's love of art. During extensive European travels he was inspired by the 'house museum' that became London's Victoria & Albert Museum. As his collection grew, Pezzoli had the idea of transforming his apartments into a series of historically themed rooms based on the great art periods of the past.*

⊙ MAP P54, A4

📞 02 79 48 89

www.museopoldipezzoli.it

Via Manzoni 12

adult/reduced €10/7

🕙 10am-6pm Wed-Mon

Ⓜ Montenapoleone

## Sala d'Armi

The armoury was the first room of Pezzoli's 'house museum' to be completed. Its neo-Gothic interiors were styled by Teatro alla Scala set designer Filippo Peroni, but his theatrical folly was destroyed in WWII. The new room, with its tomb-like interior designed by Arnaldo Pomodoro, feels like something from a 16th-century *Raiders of the Lost Ark*.

## Sala d'Artista

Following the fashionable dictates of the day, Giuseppe Bertini and Luigi Scrosati decorated the rooms of Pezzoli's apartment in different period styles in order to evoke the era of the objects on display. Of these 'Artistic Rooms' only four survived the bombing of WWII, and they have been refurbished in exquisite detail: the rococo-style Stucco Room; the Black Room, originally clad in mahogany and ivory; the Antique Murano room, Pezzoli's bedroom; and the Byzantine-influenced Dante study, where Pezzoli kept his prized possessions.

## The Collection

As a collector, Pezzoli focused on his passion for arms, the decorative arts and Renaissance paintings. Wander from room to room and admire Lombard Renaissance masters Foppa, Bergognone and Luini; Tuscan and Venetian greats including Botticelli, Bellini and Piero della Francesca in the Golden Room; and the beautiful *Portrait of a Woman* by del Pollaiolo, which is now the museum's icon. Between them you'll skirt around displays of Venetian glass, 18th-century porcelain and cabinets gleaming with jewellery.

### ★ Top Tips

o Unlike other museums, the Poldi Pezzoli is closed on Tuesdays.

o In addition to the Sala d'Artista, the museum holds Italy's finest collection of antique timepieces.

o Guided tours are available in a variety of languages and last about an hour.

o The museum is part of the Case Museo card network (adult/reduced €20/10; www.casemuseo milano.it), which offers a discount on admission to Milan's four 'house museums'.

### ✗ Take a Break

Consider a coffee at Pasticceria Marchesi (p60), the prettiest, pastel-coloured cafe in the Quad.

# Walking Tour 🚶

## Shop Like a Local

*For anyone interested in the fall of a frock or the cut of a jacket, a stroll around the Quadrilatero d'Oro, the world's most famous shopping district, is a must. This quaintly cobbled quadrangle of streets is full of Italy's most famous brands sporting fantastic window displays. Even if you don't have the slightest urge to sling a swag of glossy carriers over your arm, the people-watching is priceless.*

### Walk Facts

**Start** Via Monte Napoleone; **M** Montenapoleone

**End** Via della Spiga; **M** San Babila

**Length** 1.5km; two hours

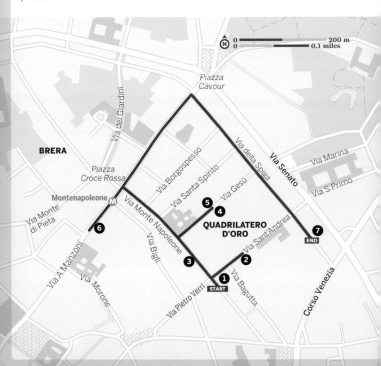

## ❶ Coffee at Cova

Coffee and cake at **Pasticceria Cova** (📞02 7600 5599, www.cova milano.com; Via Monte Napoleone 8; 🕑7.45am-8.30pm Mon-Sat, 9.30am-7.30pm Sun; Ⓜ Montenapoleone) gives you a glimpse into the glamorous world of the Quad. This is the oldest cafe in Milan, opened in 1817 by Antonio Cova, a soldier of Napoleon.

## ❷ Historic Fashion

For a glimpse of aristocratic life during the 18th century, wander around **Palazzo Morando** (📞02 8846 5735; www.costumemoda immagine.mi.it; Via Sant'Andrea 6; adult/reduced museum €5/3, exhibitions €10/8; 🕑9am-1pm & 2-5.30pm Tue-Sun; Ⓜ San Babila). Housing the personal collections of Countess Bolognini, the apartments are also hung with artworks depicting Milan during the Napoleonic era.

## ❸ Browsing 'Monte Nap'

Via Monte Napoleone has always been synonymous with elegance and money (Napoleon's government managed loans here). It is the most important street of the Quad, lined with global brands.

## ❹ Lunch at the Four Seasons

The Quad's most discreet and luxurious hotel, the Four Seasons is tucked out of sight down narrow Via Gesù. The neoclassical facade hides a 15th-century Renaissance convent complete with frescoes and a tranquil arcaded cloister. Dine here at La Veranda (p59).

## ❺ Museo Bagatti Valsecchi

Though born a few centuries too late, Fausto and Giuseppe Bagatti Valsecchi were determined to be Renaissance men, and from 1878 to 1887 they built their **home** (📞02 7600 6132; www.museobagatti valsecchi.org; Via Gesù 5; adult/reduced €9/6; 🕑1-5.45pm Tue-Sun; Ⓜ Montenapoleone) as a living museum of the Quattrocento (the cultural and artistic events of 15th-century Italy), filled with Renaissance furnishings and paintings.

## ❻ Alessi Homewares HQ

Established in Omegna in 1921, **Alessi** (📞02 79 57 26; www.alessi. com; Via Manzoni 14-16; 🕑10am-7pm; Ⓜ Montenapoleone) has crafted more than 22,000 utensils, many designed by the world's leading architect-designers. New York's MoMA features pieces, but you can find everything at this flagship store.

## ❼ Spa on Via della Spiga

Who wouldn't love shopping on pedestrianised Via della Spiga? But if the cobbles are killing your feet, take the back door into the Hotel Baglioni and check into the **Spiga 8 Spa** (📞02 7707 7454; www. baglionihotels.com; Via della Spiga 8, Hotel Baglioni; treatments from €80; 🕑10am-8pm Mon-Fri, to 7pm Sat & Sun; Ⓜ San Babila).

Quadrilatero d'Oro & Giardini Pubblici

**For reviews see**

| | | |
|---|---|---|
| ◆ | Top Experiences | p50 |
| ◉ | Sights | p55 |
| ✕ | Eating | p57 |
| 🍷 | Drinking | p60 |
| 🛍 | Shopping | p62 |

500 m
0.25 miles

Casa Museo
2 Boschi-di Stefano ◉

Via Bartolomeo Eustachi

Via Castel Morrone

Via G B Morgagni

Via Ombroni

Via Maiocchi

Via Nino Bixio

Via Nino Bixio

Via Gustavo Modena

Via Perio

Corso Buenos Aires

Via San Gregorio

Via Felice Casati

Via Melzo

13 ✕

Via Lambro

Via Frisi

Via Vallazze

Porta
Venezia

Via Alessandro Tadino

Via Panfilo Castaldi

Viale Tunisia

Via Vittorio Veneto

Bastioni di Porta Venezia

Civico Planetario
Ulrico Hoepli

Giardini
Pubblici Indro
Montanelli 5 ◉

4 ◉

Via Marina

Via Giuseppe Sirtori

Viale Piave

Porta
Venezia

20 ◉

Viale Luigi Majno

27 🛍

Piazza del
Tricolore

Corso Venezia

Galleria d'Arte
Moderna 3 ◉ 10 ◉

Via Palestro

M Palestro

Via Cappuccini

Corso Monforte

Villa Necchi
1 Campiglio ◉

Via Mozart

Stazione Centrale
(1km) ◆

Via Vitor
Pisani

Via della Moscova

Via Montebello

Via Filippo Turati

M Turati

Piazza
Cavour

Via Fatebenefratelli

Via dell'Annunciata

BRERA

Via dei Giardini

Piazza
Croce
Rossa

M Montenapoleone

Museo
Poldi
Pezzoli ◆

Via dei Giardini

36 🛍

26 🛍

Via Senato

35 🛍

33 🛍

31 🛍

17 ◉

Via Alessandro Manzoni

15

9

19 ◉

Via Gesù

Via Bigli

18

25 🛍

Via Monte Napoleone

Via Sant'Andrea

Via della Spiga

14

30 🛍

29 🛍

Via Borgospesso

12 ✕

Via San Damiano

32 🛍

Piazza
San Babila

28 🛍

Via Bagutti

34 🛍

21 🛍

Pietro Verri

Corso G Matteotti

# Sights

## Villa Necchi Campiglio
MUSEUM

**1** 🔘 MAP P54, C4

This exquisitely restored 1930s villa was designed by rationalist architect Piero Portaluppi for Pavian heiresses Nedda and Gigina Necchi, and Gigina's husband Angelo Campiglio. The trio were proud owners of one of Milan's only swimming pools, as well as terrarium-faced sunrooms and streamlined electronic shuttering. Portaluppi's commingling of art deco and rationalist styles powerfully evokes Milan's modernist imaginings while at the same time remaining anchored to a past that was rapidly slipping away. (☎ 02 7634 0121; www.visitfai.it/villanecchi; Via Mozart 14; adult/child €12/4; ⏱10am-6pm Wed-Sun; Ⓜ San Babila)

## Casa Museo Boschi-di Stefano
MUSEUM

**2** 🔘 MAP P54, E1

Milan's most eccentric museum of 20th-century Italian painting is crowded in a 1930s apartment that still has the appearance of the *haute-bourgeois* home it once was. It's a heady art hit, with Boccioni's dynamic brushstrokes propelling painting towards futurism; the nostalgically metaphysical Campigli and de Chirico; and the restless, expressionist Informels all packed into small salons decked with suitably avant-garde furnishings.

## Milan's First Skyscraper

Gio Ponti's modernist icon, the **Torre Pirelli** (Piazza Duca d'Aosta 3; Ⓜ Centrale FS), was the first building in Milan to dare to top the Madonnina on top of the Duomo. Construction on the 32-storey *grattacielo* (skyscraper) began in 1956 on the site of the company's 19th-century factory, symbolically bookending Italy's industrial heyday. The smooth tapered sides form the shape of a diamond, Ponti's oft-used graphic trademark, and still mark it out as the most elegant modern building in the city.

(☎ 02 8846 3736; www.fondazione boschidistefano.it; Via Giorgio Jan 15; admission free; ⏱10am-6pm Tue-Sun; Ⓜ Lima)

## Galleria d'Arte Moderna
GALLERY

**3** 🔘 MAP P54, C3

Napoleon's temporary Milanese home, the 18th-century Villa Reale, now houses Milan's modern art collection. Made up of bequests from leading Milanese families, the collection contains a spread of 19th- and 20th-century Italian and international art, progressing from pieces by neoclassical sculptor Canova (in the ballroom) to futurist painters Giacomo Balla and Umberto Boccioni. (GAM; ☎ 02 8844 5943; www.gam-milano.com;

Via Palestro 16; adult/reduced €5/3; ⊙9am-5.30pm Tue-Sun; MPalestro)

## Civico Planetario Ulrico Hoepli
PLANETARIUM

4 ◉ MAP P54, D2

Deep stargazing has found its place in Italy's biggest planetarium. Not only will it open your eyes to the wonders of the universe, it does so in very elegant settings. Designed by iconic Milanese architect Piero Portaluppi, the seemingly austere exterior of stone and marble is balanced with art deco touches and a playful trail of constellations as decoration. While almost all sessions are in Italian, for astronomy fans it's still well worth it. (Planetario di Milano; ☏02 8846 3340; www.comune. milano.it/planetario/; Corso Venezia

57; adult/child €5/3; ⊙sessions: 9pm Tue & Thu, 3pm & 4.30pm Sat & Sun; MPorta Venezia)

## Giardini Pubblici Indro Montanelli
GARDENS

5 ◉ MAP P54, C2

A life story unfolds as you follow pebble paths past bumper cars and a carousel, onwards past games of football, kissing teens, a beer kiosk, babies in prams, jogging paths and shady benches. Jump in, or just stop and smell the roses. For grey days, the neo-Romanesque **Museo Civico di Storia Naturale** (Natural History Museum; ☏02 8846 3337; www.comune.milano.it/museostoria naturale; Corso Venezia 55; adult/reduced €5/3; ⊙9am-5.30pm Tue-Sun; 👫; MPalestro) beckons families with quaint displays and dioramas

Casa Museo Boschi-di Stefano (p55)

of dinosaurs, fossils, fauna and the largest geology collection in Europe. (⏱6.30am-sunset; 👫👶; MPalestro)

# Eating

## Pavé
PASTRIES $

6 🍴 MAP P54, C1

Try not to argue over the *frolla al cacao*, an insanely good crumb tart filled with ganache and topped by raw chocolate nuggets. After all, it's just one of the temptations dreamed up by pastry maestros Diego, Luca and Giovanni. There's also San Franciscan sourdough, savoury brioche filled with ricotta and sundried tomatoes, and almond *kipfel* (flaky crescent-shaped pastry). (☎02 9439 2259; www.pavemilano.com; Via Casati 27; pastries €1.50-5.50, salads €6.50; ⏱8am-8pm Tue-Fri, 8.30am-7pm Sat & Sun; 📶🍴👫; MPorta Venezia)

## NÚN
KEBAB $

7 🍴 MAP P54, E1

Picking up on the demand for vegan, vegetarian and raw food, this clever contemporary kebab bar serves up hearty wraps stuffed with seasonal salads, aubergine, pomegranate and felafel. Meat eaters needn't worry though, as halal chicken is also served. Order at the counter, stipulating your preferred bread, filling and sauce, then wait to be called for collection. (☎02 9163 7315; www.nunmilano.com; Via Lazzaro Spallanzani 36; kebabs €4.50-6; ⏱noon-11pm Tue-Sun; 📶🍴; MPorta Venezia)

## Gelato Giusto
GELATO $

8 🍴 MAP P54, D1

This gelateria is a temple to Lombardy's luxurious milk products: everything here is 100% natural, handmade and locally sourced. What's more, owner Vittoria is a Maître Chocolatier constantly in search of innovative and delightful flavours such as pistachio, cinnamon and blackcurrant, and ricotta with bitter orange. (☎02 2951 0284; www.gelatogiusto.it; Via San Gregorio 17; cones €2.50-4.50; ⏱noon-8.30pm Tue-Sun; ❄👫; MPorta Venezia)

## Chic & Go
SANDWICHES $

9 🍴 MAP P54, B4

Only in the Quad: stylish fast food such as lobster *panini* (sandwiches), velouté of asparagus and saffron-scented bulgar salads. As you'd expect there's only bespoke tailoring here: choose a bread of your liking (sesame, poppy seed, bagel or baguette) then add first-class toppings such as Angus beef tartare, crabmeat mixed with paprika-spiced mayonnaise, and *mortadella* (pork cold cut) from Prato. Delicious. (☎02 78 26 48; www.chic-and-go.com; Via Bigli 20; sandwiches €5-14; ⏱8am-8pm; 🍴; MMontenapoleone)

## LùBar
SICILIAN $$

10 MAP P54, C3

This fashionable Sicilian restaurant in the 19th-century glasshouse of Napoleon's neoclassical Villa Reale is the brainchild of Luisa Beccaria's three offspring; Ludivico, Lucrezia and Lucilla. The family estate provides the table olive oil and dishes of puntarella and anchovies or fennel and orange salad arrive on beautiful ceramics from Caltagirone. (02 8352 7769; www.lubar.it; Via Palestro 16; meals €25-35; 8am-midnight Tue-Sun; M Palestro)

## Osteria del Treno
ITALIAN $$

11 MAP P54, D1

This Slow Food *osteria* (tavern) with its Liberty-style ballroom is a piece of Milanese history, built as a club for railway workers at the nearby Stazione Centrale. Self-service lunches showcase a variety of Presidio-protected cheeses, cured meats and simple, authentic pasta dishes. Dinner is a more formal affair and on Sunday nights a *milonga* (tango) takes place in the ballroom. (02 670 04 79; www.osteriadeltreno.it; Via San Gregorio 46; meals €35; 12.30-2.30pm & 8pm-1am Mon-Fri, 8pm-1am Sat & Sun; M Centrale)

## Corsia del Giardino
MODERN ITALIAN $$

Named for the gardens that once lined Via Manzoni, this contemporary cafe-restaurant, in the same building as Gallo (see 36 Map p54, A4) occupies a leafy niche off the main drag. Its sleek interior and straightforward menu match the clientele, workers from nearby shops in the Quad, who come here for top-quality salads, gourmet burgers and satisfyingly sweet fruit tarts. (02 7628 0726; www.corsiadelgiardino.it; Via Manzoni 16; meals €20-30; 8am-9pm Mon-Sat, from 9am Sun; M Montenapoleone)

## Il Baretto al Baglioni
MILANESE $$$

12 MAP P54, C4

Il Baretto's cosy, clubby atmosphere and top-notch, no-nonsense Milanese menu keep its wood-panelled dining rooms packed with silver-haired foxes and their bejewelled partners. The typical Milanese repertoire here includes not only *cotoletta* (breaded veal) and osso buco but an unforgettable white truffle risotto and *riso salto* (pan-fried risotto cakes). A not-so-secret door provides entrance from Via della Spiga 6. (02 78 12 55; www.ilbarettoalbaglioni.it; Via Senato 7; meals €60; 12.30-3pm & 7.30-11pm; M San Babila)

## Dim Sum
CHINESE $$$

13 MAP P54, E3

This first-class gourmet Chinese restaurant showcases the very best Lombard ingredients in a refined Chinese menu. The restaurant is super sleek with chef Wu

Jing on display in the glassed-in kitchen. Order broadly to sample the diverse offerings, which include Chianina beef and chives, pork and goji berries or seafood with a lime-flavoured rice wrap. (📞02 2952 2821; www.dimsummilano. com; Via Nino Bixio 29; meals €40-50; 🕐noon-2.30pm & 7-11.30pm Tue-Sun; ❄️; Ⓜ Porta Venezia)

## La Veranda
MODERN ITALIAN $$$

14 🍴 MAP P54, B4

Service in La Veranda's lovely but formal dining room within the Four Seasons hotel is disarmingly, unexpectedly warm, and the menu sings with surprisingly smart, unfussy offerings from Neapolitan chef Marco Veneruso. Artisanal products and seasonal ingredients feature and, in summer, you can sit outside in the historic cloister. (📞02 7 70 88; www.fourseasons. com/milan; Via Gesù 6/8; meals €80-90; 🕐noon-4.30pm & 7-11pm; 🅿️ ❄️ 🚫 🚹; Ⓜ Montenapoleone)

## Il Salumaio di Montenapoleone
BISTRO $$$

15 🍴 MAP P54, B4

*Prosecco* and *trofie al pesto* (Ligurian pasta twists coated in a basil, pine nut and olive oil paste) in an ivy-covered courtyard surrounded by Gucci and Dior: yep, you're in Milan. Lunch among models trying not to appear terminally bored by their banker boyfriends. The small goods and wines in the attached shop are pricey but difficult to pass up.

Il Salumaio di Montenapoleone

(☎02 7600 1123; www.ilsalumaiodi montenapoleone.it; Via Gesù 5; meals €30-60; ⏰8.30am-11pm Mon-Sat; ❄; Ⓜ Montenapoleone)

## Joia

ITALIAN $$$

16 ✖ MAP P54, C1

Known for seasonal produce and light, clean flavours, the menu at Joia is imbued with poetry (a winter dish of globe and Jerusalem artichokes with sweet black salsify and pomegranate is entitled 'Beneath a snowy white carpet'). After the meat-heavy Milanese diet, Michelin-starred Pietro Leeman's green realm is nothing short of delightful. The €40 lunch deal is great value. (☎02 2952 2124; www. joia.it; Via Panfilo Castaldi 18; tasting menus €90-130; ⏰noon-2.30pm & 7.30-11pm Mon-Sat; ❄✎; Ⓜ Porta Venezia)

# Drinking

## Bamboo Bar

BAR

17 ☕ MAP P54, B3

In a city full of designer bars, the Bamboo Bar literally raises the roof with its double-height glass bar. Black onyx floors and white leather sofas keep the focus on the incredible 360-degree panorama of the city and the expertly mixed cocktails. Order the signature Mary Caprese, made from organic vodka, tomato juice and a mozzarella mousse. (Armani Hotel; ☎02 8883 8888; www.armanihotelmilano. com; Via Manzoni 31; cocktails €18-22; ⏰11am-1am; 🛜; Ⓜ Montenapoleone)

## Pasticceria Marchesi

CAFE

18 ☕ MAP P54, B4

Decked out in baby pink, gold and peppermint green, Marchesi's Quad cafe is as easy on the eye as its pastries are on the taste buds. Inside you'll find a coffee bar and two large tearooms where brass-edged counters display a tantalising array of pralines, tarts, pastries and sweets. (☎02 7600 8238; www.pasticceriamarchesi.it; Via Monte Napoleone 9; ⏰7.30am-9pm; 🛜; Ⓜ Montenapoleone)

## Armani Privé

CLUB

19 ☕ MAP P54, A3

In the basement of the Armani superstore, this club has a Japanese–modernist aesthetic, the calm of which you'll need after the hysteria of getting in and clocking the drinks prices. Botox and blonde hair (or a dinner booking at Nobu) seems to help with the door police. (☎02 6231 2655; www. armanipriveclub.com; Via Gastone Pisoni 1; cocktails €20; ⏰11.30pm-3.30am Wed & Thu, to 4am Fri & Sat; Ⓜ Montenapoleone)

## HClub Diana

COCKTAIL BAR

20 ☕ MAP P54, D2

Secreted behind a vast leather curtain at the back of the Sheraton, *aperitivo* (pre-dinner drinks and snacks) at HClub Diana is one of Milan's most varied. Grab a freshly crushed peach bellini and lounge with the fashion pack around the low-lit garden pool

in the shade of magnolia trees.
(☎ 02 2058 2004; www.sheraton.com/
dianamajestic; Viale Piave 42, Sheraton
Diana Majestic; cocktails €13-15,
brunch €38-43; ⊙ 10.30am-1am; 🛜;
Ⓜ Porta Venezia)

## Sant'Ambroeus    CAFE

21 🚇 MAP P54, B4

This belle époque bar with its
glittering Murano chandelier and
counter full of sugary confection-
ary is something of an institution
in the Quad. It is frequented by
sharp-suited clients slugging
espresso and expensive cocktails,
and women of a certain age who
come to take tea in the salon or
pick up intricately decorated cele-
bration cakes. (☎ 02 7600 0540;
www.santambroeusmilano.it; Corso
Matteotti 7; cocktails €10; ⊙ 7.45am-
8.30pm Mon-Sat, from 8.45am Sun;
Ⓜ San Babila)

## Vinile    WINE BAR

22 🚇 MAP P54, D1

Calling all comic connoisseurs and
geeks, Vinile serves a limited-
production wine list, Italian craft
beers, and artisanal cold cuts and
crostini in the midst of an impressive collection of *Star Wars* and
Marvel memorabilia. Check out its
Facebook page for community art
and music events. (☎ 02 3651 4233;
www.vinilemilano.com; Via Tadino 17;
drinks €4-6, brunch €18; ⊙ 6.30pm-
midnight Mon & Sun, to 1am Wed
& Thu, to 2am Fri & Sat; Ⓜ Porta
Venezia)

## Underground Music Scene

A landmark of Milan's alternative scene, **Tunnel** (☎ 339
4032702; www.tunnel-milano.it; Via
Sammartini 30; €15-25; ⊙ 11pm-
5am Wed-Sat; Ⓜ Centrale) takes
its moniker as top underground
club seriously and is literally
housed in a tunnel beneath
the rail tracks of the Stazione
Centrale. Friday night's Le
Cannibale features indie acts
and electronica, while Saturday
evenings attract top DJs from
the techno scene.

## Pandenus    BAR

23 🚇 MAP P54, D1

Originally a bakery, Pandenus was
named after the walnut bread
that used to emerge from its (still
active) oven. Now the focaccia,
pizzetta and bruschetta on its
*aperitivo* bar are some of the best
in town. Given its proximity to the
Marconi Foundation (which is dedicated to contemporary art), expect
a good-looking, arty crowd. Other
branches are dotted around town.
(☎ 02 2952 8016; www.pandenus.it;
Via Tadino 15; cocktails €8-10, brunch
€20; ⊙ 7.30am-midnight Mon-Sat,
from 8am Sun; 🛜; Ⓜ Porta Venezia)

## Bar Basso    BAR

24 🚇 MAP P54, F1

This elegant corner bar is home of
the *sbagliato,* a negroni made with
*prosecco* instead of gin, as well as

## Electronic Music Revolutionaries

Like other areas of Italy, Milan had its own tradition of singer-songwriters, but it was the city's passion for classical music coupled with its engineering prowess that led to the focus on experimental music that abandoned classical concepts of melody and harmony. Chiming with the iconoclastic tendencies of the post-war Futurist movement, Italian composers began experimenting with the physical 'shape' of music and its psychological impact. This culminated, in 1955, in Luciano Berio's and Bruno Maderna's ground-breaking Studio di Fonologia Musicale (also known as RAI Milan), Italy's first centre dedicated to electronic and electroacoustic research. This fascination with electro and techno music continues today in venues like Tunnel (p61) and VOLT (p118), and the music festival Elita (www.elita.it).

the brilliant concept of *mangia e bevi* (eat and drink), involving a supersized goblet of strawberries, cream and *nocciola* (hazelnut) ice cream and a large slug of some kind of booze. It's the creatives bar of choice during Design Week. (📞 02 2940 0580; www.barbasso.com; Via Plinio 39; cocktails €7; 🕙 9am-1.15am Wed-Mon; Ⓜ Lima)

# Shopping

### Aspesi          FASHION & ACCESSORIES

**25** 🅐 MAP P54, B4

The size of this Antonio Citterio–designed shop is a clue to just how much Italians love this label – Aspesi outerwear is *de rigueur* for mountain and lake weekends, while its smart casual wear helps you segue back to city living in comfort. The arty industrial sprawl is at odds with such a practical marque: sportswear at its most

understated. (📞 02 7602 2478; www.aspesi.com; Via Monte Napoleone 13; 🕙 10am-7pm Mon-Sat; Ⓜ San Babila, Montenapoleone)

### 43 Cycles          BICYCLES

**26** 🅐 MAP P54, B3

Alberto Crivellenti's bespoke bicycle company produces the Rolls Royce of bicycles, using braze-welded steel; some have hand-sewn detailing in deerskin or alligator.

Clients come here for a totally customised cycle and everything is handmade, down to the bronze and copper bells.

Its plans for the future: to produce the first desirable electric bike, with a miniature engine developed by the Polytechnic of Milan. (📞 340 8989402; www.43cycles.com; Via Manzoni 43; 🕙 10am-7pm Mon-Sat; Ⓜ Montenapoleone)

## Imarika
CLOTHING

**27** MAP P54, D3

Fashionista Benedetta Bevilacqua seeks breakthrough designers with an eye for bold colours, unique prints and sharp shapes, which she presents with flair in this fun and friendly boutique. Her unique taste makes her a valuable personal stylist, which is why this is the perfect place to come for some true Milanese style advice. (☏02 7600 5268; www.imarika.com; Via Giovanni Morelli 1; ⊙3-7.30pm Mon, 9.30am-1.30pm & 3-7.30pm Tue-Sat; ⟨⟨9, 19)

## Larusmiani
FASHION & ACCESSORIES

**28** MAP P54, B4

Metrosexual men the world over make a beeline for chic menswear and lifestyle store Larusmiani, which is home to heritage grooming experts G. Lorenzi. Kitting out aristocratic families since 1929, Aldo Lorenzi's collection includes more than 100 styles of nail scissors, walnut cufflink boxes and chic picnic sets, all of it displayed in vintage walnut and burl wood glass-fronted cabinets. (☏02 7600 6957; www.larusmiani.it; Via Monte Napoleone 7; ⊙10am-7.30pm Mon-Sat, 10.30am-2pm & 3-7pm Sun; MMontenapoleone)

## Doriani
FASHION & ACCESSORIES

**29** MAP P54, B4

Established in 1930, Doriani is renowned for its ultrasoft cashmere knits, including polo shirts, cardigans and sweaters. Its quintessentially understated menswear is sought after by politicians, footballers and businessmen who prize the classic shapes and subtle, subdued colour palette. (☏02 7602 1527; www.doriani.it; Via Sant'Andrea 7; ⊙10am-7.30pm Mon-Sat, 10am-1.30pm & 2.30-7pm Sun; MMontenapoleone)

## Borsalino
FASHION & ACCESSORIES

**30** MAP P54, B4

Master hatter Giuseppe Borsalino apprenticed in Paris for seven years before opening his first store in 1857. Still Italy's most famous headgear, the iconic rabbit felt fedora with its natty grosgrain band is now worn by cool cats such as Denzel Washington and John Malkovich. More recently the brand has branched out into beanies and even motorcycle helmets. (☏02 7601 7072; www.borsalino.com; Via Sant'Andrea 5; ⊙10am-1pm & 2-7pm Mon-Sat; MMontenapoleone)

## Pellini
JEWELLERY, ACCESSORIES

**31** MAP P54, B3

For unique, one-off costume jewellery pieces, bags and hair pieces, look no further than the boutique of Donatella Pellini, granddaughter of famous costume designer Emma Pellini. The Pellini women have been making their trademark resin jewellery for three generations, and their fanciful creations incorporating flowers, sand and fabric are surprisingly affordable. (☏02 7600 8084; www.pellini.it; Via Manzoni 20; ⊙2.30-7.30pm Mon, from 9.30am Tue-Sat; MMontenapoleone)

Milanese fashion at Etro

## Car Shoe
SHOES

**32** MAP P54, C4

Now under the wing of Patrizio Bertelli (Mr Prada), the original '60s hybrid of sport shoe and smart casual loafer is set for a comeback in this flagship shop. To counter the lothario reputation, it now also does ranges for women and kids. (02 7602 4027; www.carshoe.com; Via della Spiga 1; 10am-7.30pm Mon-Sat, 11am-7pm Sun; San Babila)

## Sermoneta
FASHION & ACCESSORIES

**33** MAP P54, B3

A hole in the wall on chic Via della Spiga, Sermoneta's boutique store sells standards such as hand-stitched calfskin gloves alongside more unique styles made of pony skin or peccary hide. (02 7631 8303; www.sermonetagloves.com; Via della Spiga 31; 3-7pm Mon, from 10am Tue-Sat; Montenapoleone)

## Etro
FASHION, HOMEWARES

**34** MAP P54, B4

Gimmo Etro founded his fashion brand in 1968 and it's still run by the family. Contrary to the usual Milanese minimalism, Etro celebrates colour and pattern, offering checked blazers and ankle-length shearling coats that reverse to printed fabrics. The signature paisley print also appears on everything from scarves and ties to handbags and furnishings. (02 7600 5049; www.etro.it; Via Monte Napoleone 5; 10am-7.30pm; San Babila)

## DMagazine
FASHION & ACCESSORIES

**35** MAP P54, B3

Given you usually have to schlep out of town for deeply discounted designer threads, what's up with this oddly central outlet? Yes, all the major labels are here, but tend to be the stranger of their kind. However, if you dig deep, you can unearth designer finds for as little as 20% of the original retail price. (02 7600 6027; www.dmagazine. it; Via Manzoni 44; 10am-7.30pm; Montenapoleone)

## Gallo
FASHION & ACCESSORIES

**36** MAP P54, A4

Gallo may spice up its seasonal collections but it's the perennial striped knee socks in silk, cotton, wool and cashmere that locals love for adding secret colour to drab business attire. The range for men, women, children and babies is equally wide. (02 78 36 02; www.theartofgallo.it; Via Manzoni 16; 10am-7.30pm Mon-Sat, from 11am Sun; Montenapoleone)

## Habits Culti
HOMEWARES

**37** MAP P54, C3

Stuffy offices beg to be misted with Culti's green-tea room spray; their spice-spiked candles turn ordinary bathrooms into beauty temples. The savoury scents, plus dramatic flower bouquets with reed and driftwood accents, have a devoted following. (02 8398 6600; www.habitsculti.it; Corso Venezia 53; 10.30am-2pm & 3-7.30pm Tue-Sat; Palestro)

# Walking Tour 🥾

## Architectural Adventure

*Milan's grab bag of architectural styles marks the city's restless evolution into a modern metropolis, from neoclassical shopping malls and baroque palazzi (mansions) to 19th-century boulevards lined with Liberty-style apartments and rationalist villas. Take a stroll through the architectural fashions on this walk.*

### Walk Facts

**Start** Piazza del Duomo;
Ⓜ Duomo

**End** Piazza Duca d'Aosta;
Ⓜ Centrale FS

**Length** 4.5km; two hours

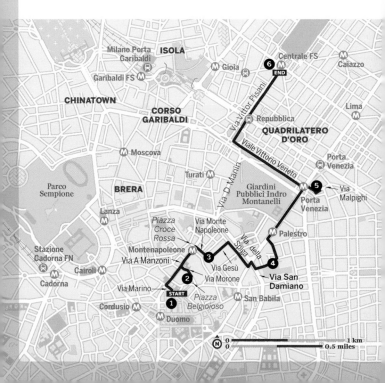

## ❶ Galleria Vittorio Emanuele II

The glass and steel gallery (p44) is the direct progenitor of the modern shopping mall. It is home to some of the oldest shops and cafes in Milan, including Camparino in Galleria (p42), founded in 1867, and **Savini**, where Charlie Chaplin declared 'I've never eaten so well'.

## ❷ Casa degli Omenoni

Wander north to Via degli Omenoni to enjoy the marvellous giants holding up the balcony of the **Casa degli Omenoni** (House of the Telamons), a 16th-century artist's residence. The vigorous Michelangelesque giants with their bulging muscles and bent backs became a reference for Milanese decorative architecture.

## ❸ Quadrilatero d'Oro

Lined with global marques, Via Monte Napoleone is the heart of the Fashion District. It was once filled with small grocers and haberdasheries, which served the stately mansions. Look out for Museo Bagatti Valsecchi (p53) with its fabulous Renaissance home decor.

## ❹ Villa Necchi Campiglio

After the Great War, Milan's architects embraced the brave new world of modernism. None more so than Piero Portaluppi, whose signature style of art deco and rationalist rigour is stamped all over town. A highlight is the Villa Necchi Campiglio (p55) which boasts a terrarium, radical electronic shutters and Milan's first domestic swimming pool.

## ❺ Casa Galimberti

Tracing the eastern boundary of the **Giardini Pubblici**, Corso Venezia is lined with neoclassical and Liberty-style palaces. On Via Malpighi, **Casa Galimberti** (Ⓜ Porta Venezia) typifies the style with its exuberant ceramic facade and twirling wrought-iron balconies.

## ❻ Torre Pirelli

End at the Mesopotamian-style **Stazione Centrale** (www.milanocentrale.it; Piazza Duca d'Aosta; Ⓜ Centrale FS). Adorned with winged horses, medallions and mosaic panelling, it is the largest train station in Italy. In answer to its fanciful art deco formula, Gio Ponti's sleek **Torre Pirelli** (1955–60) stands opposite, shooting skywards with a graceful, modern lightness.

---

### 🍴 Take a Break

Stop for a stylish cappuccino and a mini *cornetto* (croissant) at Pasticceria Cova (p53). For evening *aperitivo* (pre-dinner drinks and snacks), press on to LùBar (p58), housed in the glasshouse of the neoclassical Villa Reale.

# Explore ⊚
# Brera & Parco Sempione

*Brera's cobbled streets and ancient buildings are a reminder that Milan wasn't always a modern metropolis. At the heart of the neighbourhood is the 17th-century Palazzo di Brera, originally a Jesuit college, though occupied by the city's famous Academy of Fine Art since 1776.*

*Brera is a study in boho raffishness thanks to the academy (p72) which dominates the area. You'll no doubt want to spend the morning exploring its stunning collection of Old Masters. Then meander the cobbled streets, gallery hopping and window shopping: Via Brera, Via Solferino and Via Madonnina are some of the city's most picturesque. Stop for lunch amid the flowers in Fioraio Bianchi (p80) or graze on sizzling teppanyaki at Tokyo Grill (p78). After lunch drift westwards to Castello Sforzesco (p70) or the Triennale (p77) design museum. Early evening rewards a walk across the park up to Napoleon's magnificent Arco della Pace (p77). It looks gorgeous in the sunset and is surrounded by aperitivo bars.*

## Getting There & Around

Ⓜ For the Pinacoteca di Brera, use Montenapoleone on M3 (yellow line) and Lanza on M2 (green line); for the castle and park use Cairoli on M1 (red line) or Lanza on M2 (green line); for the Triennale, exit at Cadorna on M1 (red line) and M2 (green line).

🚃 Number 1 gives good access to the shopping street Via Vetero.

**Brera & Parco Sempione Map on p76**

Castello Sforzesco (p70) FABER1893/SHUTTERSTOCK ©

## Top Experience 📷
# Explore History at Castello Sforzesco

*This iconic red-brick castle was home to the
mighty Sforza dynasty that ruled Renaissance
Milan. The castle's defences were designed by the
multi-talented da Vinci; Napoleon later drained
the moat and removed the drawbridges. Today
it shelters seven museums, which showcase
fragments of Milan's cultural and civic history,
from the medieval equestrian tomb of Bernabò
Visconti to Michelangelo's Rondanini Pietà.*

◉ MAP P76, C3

📞 02 8846 3703

www.milanocastello.it

Piazza Castello

adult/reduced €10/8

🕙 9am-5.30pm Tue-Sun

Ⓜ Cairoli

## The Architecture

To withstand any presumptuous challenges to their power, Milan's politicking Sforzas (1447–1500) gave the castle its robust medieval character. Francesco invited Florentine architect, Filarete, to design the high central tower in 1452 to give the effect of an elegant residence rather than a barracks. Thick round towers, faced with diamond-shaped *serizzo,* bolstered the ramparts. Inside, the ducal apartments were endowed with elegant pavilion vaults, and were later decorated by Leonardo da Vinci.

## Musei d'Arte Antica

Housed in the frescoed ducal apartments, the Museum of Ancient Art has a stellar medieval collection. From paleo-Christian frescoes to the fine equestrian tomb of Bernarbò Visconti, the artworks relate the ambitious story of Italy's first city *comune.* Da Vinci frescoed the octagonal ceiling of the Sala delle Asse (room VIII) while in room VI is the tremendous Gonfalcon (ensign) of Milan, depicting St Ambrose embroidered in gold thread, pearls and rubies.

## Rondanini Pietà

Michelangelo's *Rondanini Pietà* is his final, and some say finest, piece of work. Depicting Mary struggling to support the dying Christ, it has an exaggerated simplicity, which many think makes it the earliest piece of modern art, although it was unfinished at his death in 1564.

## Museo dei Mobile and Pinacoteca

The Furniture Museum and castle Art Gallery blend seamlessly, leading you from ducal wardrobes and writing desks through to a blockbuster collection of Lombard Gothic art. Among the masterpieces are Andrea Mantegna's *Trivulzio Madonna,* Vicenzo Foppa's *St Sebastian* and Bramantino's *Noli me tangere (Touch me not).*

★ **Top Tips**

o Admission to the museums is free on Tuesday from 2pm, and every first Sunday of the month.

o Highly recommended is the tour of the castle's battlements and underground rooms with **Ad Artem** (www.adartem. it; Via Melchiorre Gioia 1; adult €13-20, child €8; 👶; Ⓜ Sondrio).

o If you're short on time, the best collection is the Musei d'Arte Antica (Museum of Ancient Art), and Michelangelo's *Rondanini Pietà* is unmissable.

✕ **Take a Break**

If the weather's nice, have a drink on the terrace of **Bar Bianco** (www. bar-bianco.com; Parco Sempione; ⊙ 9am-1am Mon-Thu & Sun, to 2am Fri & Sat summer, 10am-6pm winter; 🛜 👶 👪; Ⓜ Lanza).

For something more hearty, try elegant Rovello 18 (p78).

## Top Experience 📷

# Wander the Masterpiece-Packed Halls of Pinacoteca di Brera

*Located upstairs from the Brera Academy, this gallery houses Milan's collection of Old Masters, much of it 'lifted' by Napoleon during his Italian campaigns. Rembrandt, Goya and van Dyck all have a place in the collection, but you're here to see the Italians. Much of the work has tremendous emotional clout, most notably Mantegna's Lamentation over the Dead Christ.*

⊙ MAP P76, E3

📞 02 72 26 31

www.pinacotecabrera.org

Via Brera 28

adult/reduced €10/7

🕗 8.30am-7.15pm Tue-Wed & Fri-Sun, to 10.15pm Thu

Ⓜ Lanza, Montenapoleone

## Lombard Frescoes

The Brera collection starts with a blast of Renaissance brilliance, launching you down a corridor lined with Donato Bramante's *Men at Arms* and Bernardino Luini's frescoes from the suppressed church of La Pace and Casa Pelucca. While Luini's tableau of girls playing 'hot-cockles' illustrates the influence of Leonardo da Vinci in its blending of Renaissance innovations with indigenous Milanese scenes, Bramante's soldiers define a new understanding of illusionistic perspective. In room IA is a reconstruction of the 14th-century oratory of Mocchirolo and its splendid fresco cycle, thought to be the work of Giotto.

## Bellini & Mantegna

The works of Giovanni Bellini and Andrea Mantegna, displayed in room VI, are some of the highlights of the Pinacoteca's Venetians. Like Bramante before him, Mantegna had a passion for rigorous perspective and a love of classicism that combined to create the stunningly unsentimental *Lamentation over the Dead Christ,* with its violent foreshortening of Christ's corpse. Although influenced by Mantegna, Bellini's sad-eyed Madonnas and exquisitely tender *Pietà* demonstrate the progressing humanisation of the subject, enhanced by the expressive effects of colour and light in the landscape around them.

## Titian, Tintoretto & Veronese

The high-water mark of the Renaissance dawned in Venice in the 16th century with an extraordinary confluence of talent in the persons of Tizian Vercelli (Titian), Jacopo Tintoretto and Paolo Veronese. While Rome was in decline and the rest of Italy oppressed by moral mores that the licentious Venetians scoffed at, Venice had both the deep pockets of the Doge and his stabilising iron rule. So wealth, patronage and art

★ **Top Tips**

o You'll need at least half a day to cover the gallery's 38 rooms at a reasonable pace.

o Audioguides are available in Italian, French, English, Spanish and German for €5.

o Every Thursday evening, from 6pm to 10pm, entrance to the gallery is just €3; and on every third Thursday live music is performed throughout the gallery.

✕ **Take a Break**

Drop into Tokyo Grill (p78), just around the corner, for a plate of delicious seared *teppanyaki*.

Stroll north through Brera's picturesque streets for a superior glass of wine at N'Ombra de Vin (p81).

## Understanding the Collection

Napoleon amassed Brera's masterpieces from all over Lombardy, the Veneto, Emilia and Le Marche with the specific intention of creating 'the Louvre of Italy'. Organised as a journey through time and space, the gallery's 38 rooms proceed chronologically from the 13th to the 20th century, examining different regional schools and styles and offering the visitor a unique insight into Italian culture over the centuries.

flourished, with Titian as protagonist. Room IX brings together some of the period's greatest works, including Titian's *St Jerome* and Veronese's *Cena in casa di Simone (Dinner at Simone's House)*.

## The Urbino School

One of the greatest painters of the early Renaissance, Piero della Francesca was engaged by Urbino's Count of Montefeltro in 1474. Although the Tuscan artist and mathematician is more famous for his cycle of frescoes depicting the Legend of the True Cross in Arezzo's Basilica di San Francesco, the monumental Montefeltro altarpiece, otherwise known as the *Brera Madonna*

## Pinacoteca Di Brera

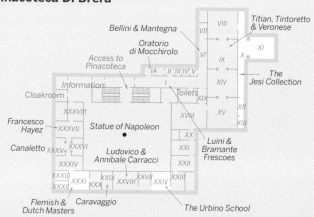

## Palazzo Citterio

After a 40-year, €23 million restoration effort, this 18th-century palace opened in 2019 as Brera's new modernist wing. Its awesome 6500 sq metres of frescoed halls, 1970s additions and vast concrete bunker is the cumulative work of a roster of august architects including Giancarlo Ortelli, Edoardo Sianesi, Franco Russoli and James Stirling (who died during the project). It is connected to the main gallery via the newly restored Orto Botanico, where a sculpture by Mimmo Paladino, the *Longobard Wall,* has been created from the rubble of the palace's decades-long restoration.

(1472–74), is the prize of room XXIV. As a counterpoint, take a look at Raphael's much looser and more natural *Wedding of the Virgin,* which was painted in 1504.

## Caravaggio

Influenced by the darkening palette and glimmering colours of the baroque Emilian school of the late 16th and early 17th centuries, room XXIX delivers an unexpected emotional thump. Home to the academy's only Caravaggio, *Cena in Emmaus (Supper at Emmaus),* the room is dark and brooding. Gone is the neat formal classicism of Raphael and the mannerist trickery of Carracci, and in its place is a potent, weighty naturalism, framed by an existential conflict between light and dark.

## Flemish Masters

Amid its huge Italian collection, the academy inherited a small selection of Flemish and Dutch masters, now housed in rooms XXXI and XXXIII. Rubens, Van Dyck and Jan

Fyt arrived from the Louvre in 1813 and in 1855 Peter Oggioni donated masters of the Antwerp school, including Jan de Beer, along with German artists Herman Rode and Hans Memling. Seen in the context of all that has gone before, the cross-pollination from the Renaissance is particularly noticeable.

## The 19th Century

By the time you reach the final rooms and the early 19th century, at which time the gallery itself was gaining prominence, the artwork becomes lighter, imbued with the romanticism and patriotism of a unified Italy. Breeze through Canaletto's atmospheric views of Venice to Francesco Hayez, pet portrait artist for the Lombard nobility and a director at the academy. His works include the intense and luminous *Il bacio (The Kiss;* 1859), one of the most reproduced artworks in the gallery, which came to symbolise the hopes of the Risorgimento (reunification period).

Brera & Parco Sempione

76

**For reviews see**
- Top Experiences p70
- Sights p77
- Eating p78
- Drinking p81
- Entertainment p81
- Shopping p82

Bastioni di Porta Venezia

Via Appiani

Piazzale Primipessa Clothilde

Via Parini

Via San Marco

Via Solferino

Via Marsala

Via della Moscova

Via Statuto

Via Palermo

Largo La Foppa

Moscova

Corso Garibaldi

Bastioni di Porta Volta

Via Legnano

Via Bramante

Viale Elvezia

Via Luigi Canonica

Arena Civica

Parco Sempione

Piazza Sempione

Arco della Pace

Triennale di Milano

Viale Emilio Alemagna

Via Mario Pagano

Via Giacomo Leopardi

Via Vincenzo Monti

Via Giovanni Boccaccio

Castello Sforzesco

Studio Museo Achille Castiglioni

Stazione Cadorna (Stazione Nord)

Piazza Castello

Foro Buonaparte

Cadorna

Cairoli

Via G. Sacchi

Via Cusani

Via Broletto

Corso di Porta Nuova

Via Principe Amedeo

Via Montebello

Via Cernaia

Palazzo Parigi Grand Spa

Via Fatebenefratelli

Via dell'Annunciata

Pinacoteca di Brera

BRERA

Via Ponte Vetero

Via Mercato

Via Fiori Chiari

Via Fiori Oscuri

Via del Santo Sepolcro

Via dei Cavalieri

Tonsor Club

Via Senato

Via della Spiga

Via Sant'Andrea

Montenapoleone

Via Alessandro Manzoni

Via dei Giardini

Via Bigli

Bulgari Spa

Via Monte di Pietà

Via Brera

Via G Verdi

Via Madonnina

Via Pontaccio

Lanza

Via Palestro

0 500 m
0 0.25 miles

# Sights

### Triennale di Milano    MUSEUM

1  MAP P76, B3

Italy's first Triennale took place in 1923 in Monza. It aimed to promote Italian design and applied arts, and its success led to the construction of Giovanni Muzio's **Palazzo d'Arte** in Milan in 1933. Since then, this exhibition space has championed design in all its forms, although the triennale formula has been replaced by long annual exhibits and international shows. (www.triennaledesign museum.it; Viale Emilio Alemanga 6; adult/reduced €9/7.50; ☉10.30am-8.30pm Tue-Sun; P; M Cadorna)

### Parco Sempione    PARK

2  MAP P76, B2

Situated behind Castello Sforzesco, Parco Sempione was once the preserve of hunting Sforza dukes. Then Napoleon came to town and set about landscaping. First the French carved out orchards; next they mooted the idea in 1891 for a vast public park. It was a resounding success and today Milanese of all ages come to enjoy its winding paths and ornamental ponds. Giò Ponti's 1933 steel **tower** (☏02 331 41 20; €5; ☉3-7pm & 8.30pm-midnight Tue, Thu & Fri, 10.30am-12.30pm & 3pm-midnight Wed, 10.30am-2pm & 2.30pm-midnight Sat & Sun summer, closes 6.30pm winter; M Cadorna) provides a fantastic 108m-high viewing platform over the park. (☉6.30am-nightfall; 🚹; M Cadorna, Lanza)

### Arco della Pace    LANDMARK

3  MAP P76, A2

Situated at the northwestern edge of Parco Sempione is Napoleon's 25m-high triumphal arch. Designed by Luigi Cagnola in 1807, it echoes Paris' Arc de Triomphe and marks the start of Corso Sempione, the main road that connects Milan to Paris via the Simplon (Sempione) Pass. Ironically, thanks to Napoleon's fall in 1814, its neoclassical facade was finished in 1838 with bas-reliefs not of Napoleon's victories, as was intended, but with scenes from the Battle of Leipzig (1813), depicting his defeat. (Piazza Sempione; M Moscova, Cairoli)

### Biking Around Brera

One of the best ways to explore Brera and the beautiful Parco Sempione is on your own set of wheels. At **Rossignoli** (☏02 80 49 60; www.rossignoli.it; Corso Garibaldi 71; bike rental 1 day/week €12/65; ☉2.30-7.30pm Mon, 9am-12.30pm & 2.30-7.30pm Tue-Sat; M Moscova), four generations of family have been kitting out Milan's cycling needs since 1926. You'll find everything here, from cute bells and baskets to top-of-the-range racing bikes. You can also hire bikes and sign up for city tours (book a few days in advance).

## Studio Museo Achille Castiglioni

MUSEUM

4 ⊙ MAP P76, B4

Architect, designer and teacher Achille Castiglioni was one of Italy's most influential 20th-century thinkers. This is the studio where he worked until his death in 2002, and the hour-long tours vividly illuminate his playful creative process. Details abound: job folders printed with specially produced numerical stamps; scale models of his Hilly sofa designed for Cassina; and a host of inspirational objects, from joke glasses to bicycle seats. (📞02 805 36 06; www.fondazioneachillecastiglioni. it; Piazza Castello 27; adult/reduced €10/7; ⏰tours 10am, 11am & noon Tue-Fri, 6.30pm, 7.30pm & 8.30pm Thu; Ⓜ Cadorna)

# Eating

## Salumeria Le Tre Regioni

SANDWICHES $

5 ⊗ MAP P76, D2

Don't miss this narrow shop front for inside lies a superb family-run deli where you can compile a lip-smacking sandwich from quality cold cuts and a good selection of Lombard cheeses. Juice, beer and bottles of wine are also for sale, and you'll often find people gathered outside at 6pm enjoying an impromptu aperitivo. (📞320 6940909; Via Palermo 16; sandwiches €3-5; ⏰8am-7.30pm Tue-Sat; Ⓜ Moscova)

## L'Orto di Brera

VEGETARIAN $

6 ⊗ MAP P76, D3

The colourful vegetables at this local grocers line the cobbled alley of San Carpoforo like floral displays at a high-end florist. Step inside and you'll find a surprising dining spot with fresh vegetal creations from chef Claudio Crotti ready to take away or snack on amid the baskets. There's also a range of freshly squeezed juices and biodynamic wines. (www.ortodibrera.com; Via San Carpoforo 6; meals €5-10; ⏰8am-2pm Mon, to 7pm Tue-Sat; 🛜 📶; Ⓜ Lanza)

## Rovello 18

OSTERIA $$

7 ⊗ MAP P76, D3

Take heart from the dresser stacked with venerable bottles of Barolo as you enter this unpretentious osteria (tavern). It's an indication of the smart, unfussy, quality food that Michele de Liguoro serves up. Fried polenta with salami or artichokes and shrimp precede plates of homemade pasta with guanciale (pork cheek) and baked rabbit. The latter pairs nicely with the Barolo. (📞02 7209 3709; www.rovello18.it; Via Tivoli 2; meals €35-50; ⏰12.30-3pm & 7-11pm Mon-Fri, 7-11pm Sat & Sun; Ⓜ Lanza)

## Tokyo Grill

JAPANESE $$

8 ⊗ MAP P76, E3

The elegant proportions of this 17th-century palazzo (mansion) fit this discreet teppanyaki restaurant close to the Brera art gallery. Downstairs, chef Gianmaria Zanotti cooks on a huge rectangular pan in front of 24 diners, while upstairs individual tables are kitted out with personal grills for do-it-yourself *yakiniku* (barbecue). (☎02 8909 2635; www.tokyogrill.it; Via Fiori Oscuri 3; meals €15-80; ⏱noon-3pm & 7.30-11pm Tue-Sun; Ⓜ Turati, Lanza)

## Volemose Bene OSTERIA $$

9 🍴 MAP P76, E2

Deliberately kitsch, rustic interiors – checked tablecloths, strings of garlic, straw flagons – a loud crush of diners and excellent Roman cooking are the ingredients of this restaurant, which lives up to its name (roughly translated as 'caring for each other'). Don't miss Jewish-style artichokes, roast lamb with potatoes or fiery *pasta all'amatriciana* (pasta with spicy tomato sauce, *pecorino* cheese and bacon). (☎02 3655 9618; www.volemosebenemilano.it; Via della Moscova 25; meals €30-35; ⏱noon-4pm & 7.30pm-2.30am; Ⓜ Moscova)

## Latteria di San Marco TRATTORIA $$

10 🍴 MAP P76, D2

If you can snare a seat in this tiny and ever-popular restaurant, you'll find old favourites such as *maccheroni al pomodoro e burro* (pasta with tomatoes and butter) mixed in with chef Arturo's own creations, such as his lemony meatballs or *riso al salto* (risotto fritters), on the daily-changing menu. Cash only. (☎02 659 76 53; Via San Marco 24; meals €35-40; ⏱12.30-2.30pm & 7.30-10pm Mon-Fri; Ⓜ Moscova)

Triennale di Milano (p77)

GIANLUCA DI IOIA - COURTESY TRIENNALE DI MILANO ©

## Grooming Gods

**Palazzo Parigi Grand Spa** (Map p76, F2; 📞 02 6256 2300; www.palazzo parigi.com; Corso di Porta Nuova 1; treatments from €90, all-day access €100; 🕘9am-9pm; M Turati) Lavish rooftop spa with a full-length pool, fitness club and pink marble hammam.

**Tonsor Club** (Map p76, D2; 📞 02 4953 3040; www.tonsorclub.com; Via Palermo 15; cuts & treatments €10-43; 🕘11am-8pm Tue-Fri, 10am-7pm Sat; M Moscova) Retro-style barber offering tonal shaves, face massages and some of the sharpest haircuts in the city.

**Bulgari Spa** (Map p76, E3; 📞 02 805 805 200; www.bulgarihotel.com; Via Privata Fratelli Gabba 7b; treatments from €80; 🕘7.30am-9pm; M Montenapoleone) Antonio Citterio's sleek, gold-lined spa offers treatments utilising exclusive La Mer, Amala and Sothys products.

## Seta

GASTRONOMY $$$

11 🍴 MAP P76, E4

Smooth as the silk after which it is named, Seta is Michelin-starred dining at its best: beautiful, inventive and full of flavour surprises. Diners sit on their teal-coloured velvet chairs in keen anticipation of Antonio Guida's inspired dishes such as plum-coloured roe deer with a splash of mango salsa. It's both rooted in tradition and subtly daring, just like Milan. (Mandarin Oriental; 📞 02 8731 8897; www. mandarinoriental.com; Via Andegari 9; meals €120; 🕘12.30-2.30pm & 7.30-10.30pm Mon-Fri, 7.30-10.30pm Sat; P ❄ 🛜; M Montenapoleone)

## Fioraio Bianchi Caffè

ITALIAN, FRENCH $$$

12 🍴 MAP P76, E2

This former florist's shop is great for a light French-influenced lunch, or an excellent *aperitivo* (pre-dinner drink) among the flowers. Dinners are fresh and inventive with particularly delicious border-crossing desserts, from Provençal lavender brûlée to a spice-inflected apple strudel. ( 📞 02 2901 4390; www.fioraiobianchicaffe.it; Via Montebello 7; meals €45-60; 🕘8am-midnight Mon-Sat; 🛜; M Turati)

## Ristorante Solferino

MILANESE $$$

13 🍴 MAP P76, E1

Salivary glands have worked overtime here for a century, thanks to hearty classics such as osso buco swathed in risotto, unexpected delights such as fish tortelloni, and an extensive vegetarian menu. Join Milanese risking their figures with the in-house pastry chef's creations, and journalists steadily losing their objectivity over a superior wine selection. ( 📞 02 2900 5748;

www.ilsolferino.com; Via Castelfidardo 2; meals €45-60; ⊙noon-2.30pm & 7-11.30pm; ❄🍴; MMoscova)

# Drinking

## Dry
COCKTAIL BAR

14 🚇 MAP P76, D1

The brainchild of Michelin-starred chef Andrea Berton, Dry pairs its cocktails with gourmet pizzas. The inventive cocktail list includes the Corpse Reviver (London Dry Gin, Cointreau, Cocchi Americano and lemon juice) and the Martinez (Boompjes Genever, vermouth, Maraschino liqueur and Boker's bitters), the latter inspired by French gold hunters in Martinez, the birthplace of barman Jerry Thomas. (📞02 6379 3414; www.drymilano.it; Via Solferino 33; cocktails €8-13, meals €20-25; ⊙7pm-1.30am Tue-Sun; 🛜; MMoscova)

## Baladin Milano
BAR

15 🚇 MAP P76, E1

At the end of super-chic Via Solferino you'll find this lovely gastropub where Piedmontese brewer Teo Musso serves his line of Baladin craft beers alongside a menu of Fassone beef burgers and sweet paprika chips. There are over 30, mainly Italian, craft beers as well as a non-alcoholic Baladin cola made using Slow Food–approved cola nuts from Sierra Leone. (www.baladin.it; Via Solferino 56; ⊙noon-3pm Mon, noon-3pm & 6-11.30pm Tue-Fri, 6pm-1am Sat; 🛜🐾; MMoscova)

## N'Ombra de VIn
WINE BAR

16 🚇 MAP P76, E3

This *enoteca* (wine bar) is set in a one-time Augustine refectory. Tastings can be had all day and you can also indulge in food such as *carpaccio di pesce spade agli agrumi* (swordfish carpaccio prepared with citrus) from a limited menu. Check the website for occasional cultural events and DJ nights. (www.nombradevin.it; Via San Marco 2; ⊙10am-2am Sun-Wed, to 3am Thu-Sat; 🛜; MLanza, Moscova)

## Radetzky Cafe
BAR

17 🚇 MAP P76, D1

Fabulous banquette and window seating make Radetzky one of the most popular *aperitivo* places on this stylish, pedestrianised strip. In keeping with the Russian theme, the menu includes smoked salmon, oysters and the exclusive Italian caviar Adamas. Sunday brunch is also served. (www.radetzky.it; Corso Garibaldi 105; ⊙7am-2am; MMoscova)

# Entertainment

## Piccolo Teatro Strehler
THEATRE

18 ⭐ MAP P76, C3

This trailblazing theatre with seating for 960 people was designed by Marco Zanuso in 1998 to address the size constraints of the original Piccolo Teatro. It has since gone on to become one of Milan's cultural powerhouses, and includes the **Teatro Studio** at Via Rivoli 6. (☎02 4241 1889; www.piccoloteatro.org; Largo Greppi 1; MLanza)

# Shopping

### F. Pettinaroli STATIONERY

19 🔒 MAP P76, D3

One of Milan's most historic outfits (with a plaque to prove it), Pettinaroli has been furnishing the city's best desks and purses since 1881 with luxe monogrammed stationery, leather-bound diaries and hand-stitched purses. Cartography buffs will love their antique maps and desk globes and if you're buying a gift, personalise it with their calligraphy service or a hand-stamped monogram. (www.fpettinaroli.it; Via Brera 4; ⏱3-7pm Mon, from 10am Tue-Sat; MMontenapoleone)

### Cavalli e Nastri FASHION & ACCESSORIES

20 🔒 MAP P76, D4

This gorgeously colourful shop is known for its vintage clothes and accessories. It specialises in lovingly curated frocks, bags, jewellery and even shoes, sourced from early- and mid-20th-century Italian fashion houses, and priced accordingly. You'll find its **menswear store** (Via Gian Giacomo Mora 3; ⏱10.30am-7.30pm Tue-Sat, 3.30-7.30pm Mon; 🚋2, 14) at Via Mora 3. (www.cavallienastri.com; Via Brera 2; ⏱10.30am-7.30pm Mon-Sat, from noon Sun; MMontenapoleone)

### Il Cirmolo VINTAGE

21 🔒 MAP P76, D3

Sourcing antiques and funky vintage artefacts since the 1960s, Il Cirmolo is a little treasure trove of joy. You can spend a whole morning here picking through period signage, weird anatomical models, lamps, friezes and even the odd car fender or two. Don't be surprised if you leave with a life-sized Betty Boop. (☎02 805 28 85; www.ilcirmoloantiquariato.it; Via Fiori Chiari 3; ⏱3-7pm Mon, from 10am Tue-Sat; MLanza)

### Rigadritto GIFTS & SOUVENIRS

22 🔒 MAP P76, E4

Loads of little stickers, clips, pencils and decorated stationery fill this graphic, colourful space, so much so that it's rather hard to 'behave' as the store name advises. Without meaning to, you'll find yourself leaving with vintage cars, pencil cases shaped like football boots, wind-up toys and fanciful pop-out cards. (☎02 8058 2936; Via Brera 6; ⏱10.30am-7.30pm Mon-Sat, 11am-7pm Sun; 👪; MMontenapoleone)

### CB Made in Italy SHOES

23 🔒 MAP P76, D2

If you can't face the teetering heels modelled in the Quadrilatero d'Oro, opt for Cecilia Bringheli's handmade loafers in a rainbow range of soft suede, hole-punched leather and bright and breezy fabric prints. Made by Lombard craftsmen, they are the perfect summer shoe: comfortable, stylish and fun. You'll find it tucked at the back of a courtyard off Corso Garibaldi. (📞02 3663 9181; www. cbmadeinitaly.com; Corso Garibaldi 50; ⏰9.30am-6.30pm Mon-Fri, 10.30am-7pm Sat; Ⓜ Moscova)

## Malìparmi   FASHION & ACCESSORIES

**24** 🔒 MAP P76, E2

It all began in Padua with Marol Paresi combining her love of travel and her craft skills to create ethnically inspired and artfully beaded, embroidered and printed bags, sandals, jewellery and clothes. Now, with her daughter beside her, she has shops around the world, but her most colourful creations are still to be found here, close to home. (📞02 7209 3899; www.mali parml.lt; Via Solferino 3; ⏰3-7pm Mon, from 10am Tue-Sat; Ⓜ Moscova)

## The Slowear Store   FASHION & ACCESSORIES

**25** 🔒 MAP P76, D2

Slowear takes its cue from the Slow Food philosophy and markets an ethical stable of menswear labels (Incotex, Zanone) that fit a wearable, timeless and tactile bill. Aside from the beautifully made clothes, you can shop around for some excellent vinyl, Carlo Moretti Venetian glasswear, elegant sunnies, polished leather wallets and cool moped helmets. (📞02 6347 1384; www.slowear.com; Via Solferino 18; ⏰10.30am-7.30pm Mon-Sat, 11am-8pm Sun; Ⓜ Moscova)

F. Pettinaroli's stationery store

# Explore

# Porta Garibaldi & Isola

*Home to César Pelli's shard-like skyscraper, Herzog & de Meuron's contemporary 'greenhouse' and Stefano Boeri's apartment blocks festooned with hanging gardens, the area between Porta Garibaldi and Porta Nuova is Milan's mini-Manhattan. Swanky Corso Como links Corso Garibaldi with the hip neighbourhood of Isola, making this a hot spot for bars, restaurants and cutting-edge shops.*

Start the day with a tour of Milan's Cimitero Monumentale (p89). Begun in 1866 by Carlo Maciachini, the cemetery has evolved into a surreal open-air museum of fashionable mausoleums. Just south of the cemetery is Chinatown, one of the most multicultural corners of Milan. It's a great place for lunch or you can wander east to the more glitzy environs of Porta Garibaldi, where you'll find food emporium Eataly (p92). In the afternoon, visit Piazza Gae Aulenti (p89), where you can admire Milan's glassy skyscrapers before crossing the park into Isola. Bar hop down Via Pastrengo and Via Thaon di Revel before nabbing a seat at the latest must-visit ramen joint.

## Getting There & Around

Ⓜ For the cemetery and the nightlife along Corso Como, exit at Garibaldi on the M2 (green line) and M5 (lilac line); for Isola continue on the M5 (lilac line), which has convenient stops at Isola and Zara.
🚋 Trams 2, 4 and 33 are useful for the cemetery, and number 33 continues to Isola.

**Porta Garibaldi & Isola Map on p88**

# Walking Tour 🥾

## A Weekend Stroll

*North of Porta Nuova's skyscrapers is Isola – an island both by name and nature, hemmed in by Porta Garibaldi's railway tracks. A postwar, working-class neighbourhood, Isola has a strong sense of community and its modest Liberty-style apartment blocks are home to a vibrant scene of artists, students and immigrants. Come on Saturday for the market or Sunday for brunch.*

### Walk Facts

**Start** Via Carlo de Cristoforis; Ⓜ Garibaldi FS

**End** Via Pollaiuolo; Ⓜ Isola

**Length**: 2.1km; two hours

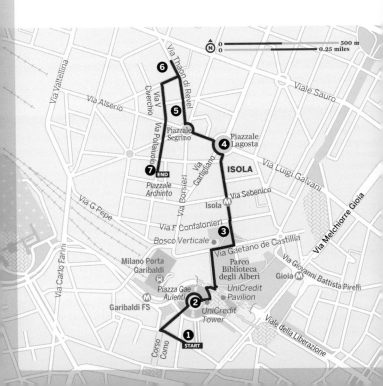

# ❶ Chocolate Treats

Start on the southside of the tracks at historic Zaini (p95), Milan's home-brand chocolatier, opened in 1913 and still located on the site of the original chocolate factory.

# ❷ Admiring Modern Milan

Join locals in exploring Piazza Gae Aulenti (p89). It is surrounded by glittering skyscrapers, including César Pelli's UniCredit Tower and Michele de Lucchi's pod-like Uni-Credit Pavilion; while north, across the park, is Stefano Boeri's Bosco Verticale.

# ❸ Casa della Memoria

Milan's **House of Memory** (☏02 8844 4102; www.casadellamemoria. it; Federico Confalonieri 14; admission free; ⏰9am-5pm Mon-Fri, 10am-6pm Sat & Sun; Ⓜ Isola) is a museum and archive commemorating citizens whose lives were lost to wars, terrorism and civic struggles. By day, you can make out the faces of 19 victims on the pixelated brick exterior, a clever visual trick suggesting the time needed to understand complex social events.

# ❹ To Market, to Market

Saturday is market day at the covered municipal market in **Piazzale Lagosta**. There are no supermarkets or shopping centres in Isola, so everyone comes here to buy their week's groceries.

# ❺ Via Thaon di Revel

Given its strong social roots, Isola is full of subcultures, not least a big biker community. This congregates along Via Thaon di Revel where you'll find dozens of cool biker shops, bars and the epic bike emporium Deus Ex Machina (p95).

# ❻ Santuario di Santa Maria alla Fontana

For centuries ailing Milanese would trek out to Isola to bathe in healing thaumaturgical pools. When French military governor Charles d'Amboise received a cure in 1507, he ordered this **sanctuary** (☏02 688 70 59; www.parrocchiafon tana.it; Piazza Santa Maria alla Fontana 11; admission free; ⏰8am-noon & 3-7pm; Ⓜ Zara) with frescoed cloisters be built over the water. The highlight is the frescoed *sacellum* (shrine), which looks like a pimped-up Roman hammam.

# ❼ Streets of Art

Finally, wander down **Via Pollaiuolo** and **Via Carmagnola** to admire some of Milan's best street art by artists like Zibe, Ozmo and Pao. Until recently, graffiti was considered vandalism in Milan and much has been painted over, but Isola's live-and-let-live vibe means much work survives here. Not least the fantastic piece on local hub Frida (p93), where you should end with a drink.

## For reviews see

| | | |
|---|---|---|
| ◎ | Sights | p89 |
| ✗ | Eating | p89 |
| 🍷 | Drinking | p92 |
| ✦ | Entertainment | p94 |
| 🛍 | Shopping | p94 |

500 m
0.25 miles

Via Giulio Cesare Procaccini

Via Schiaparelli

Via Sondrio

Via Ponte Seveso

Via Sammartini

Piazza di Savoia

Via Don Vittruvio

Via Mauro Macchi

Via Luigi Settembrini

Piazza Duca d'Aosta

Centrale FS

Via Napo Torriani

Via Tonale

Via Copernico

Via Luigi Galvani

Via Vittor Pisani

Via Fabio Filzi

Via San Gregorio

Via Felice Casati

Viale Tunisia

Viale Sauro

Viale Resteilli

Via Melchiorre Gioia

Via Generale Gustavo Fara

Via Giovanni Battista Pirelli

Republica

Via G Galilei

Viale Zara

Viale F Arese

Piazzale Lagosta

ISOLA

Via Pola

Palazzo Lombardia

Via Sebenico

Isola

Biblioteca Gioia

Piazza Alvar Aalto 8

Viale della Liberazione

Porta Nuova

Via Thaon di Revel

21 🛍 23 🛍

Piazzale Segrino 19 ✦

Via Borsieri

Via Confalonieri

Bosco Verticale Towers

Via Gaetano de Castillia

24 ◎

degli Alberi

Piazza Gae Aulenti 2

Piazza Gae Aulenti

Via Bottraffio

Via Cola Montano

Piazza Fidia 4 🍷

16 ✗

Piazzale Archinto

5 ✗

15 ✗

Via Carlo de Cristofons

Via Farini

Via A. della Pergola

Via G Pepe

Via Jacopo dal Verme

Via Pastrengo

Milano Porta Garibaldi

Garibaldi FS

22 🍷

10 🍷

Corso Como

Piazzale XXV Aprile

Eataly

Bastioni di Porta Nuova

Via Carmagnola

Via Tazzoli

Via Alessio di Tocqueville

PORTA GARIBALDI

Via F Crispi

Via Alessandro Volta

Corso Garibaldi

Via Valtellina

Via Carlo Farini

Via Ceresio

Viale Pasubio

9 🛍

3 🛍 ✦

Fondazione Feltrinelli

Bastioni di Porta Volta

Viale Montello

Cimitero Monumentale

Piazzale Cimitero Monumentale

◎ 1

14 ✗

Via Ceresio

CHINATOWN

Via Donato Bramante

13 🛍

Via Paolo Sarpi

12 🛍

6 ✗

20 ✦

Via Messina

18 ✗ 🛍

# Sights

## Cimitero Monumentale

CEMETERY

1 ⊙ MAP P88, A3

Behind striking Renaissance-revival black-and-white walls, Milan's wealthy have kept their dynastic ambitions alive long after death with grand sculptural gestures since 1866. Nineteenth-century death-and-the-maiden eroticism gives way to some fabulous abstract forms from mid-century masters. Studio BBPR's geometric steel-and-marble memorial to Milan's WWII concentration-camp dead sits in the centre, stark and moving. The tombs are divided into three zones: Catholics lie centre stage, while people of Jewish descent rest on the right and non-Catholics on the left. Grab a map inside the forecourt. (☏02 8844 1274; Piazzale Cimitero Monumentale; admission free; ⊙8am-6pm Tue-Sun; Ⓜ Monumentale)

## Piazza Gae Aulenti

ARCHITECTURE

2 ⊙ MAP P88, C3

Join locals sightseeing at this landmark square named after Italy's most famous female architect. The linchpin of Milan's Porta Nuova regeneration project, the piazza curves around a huge reflecting pool and is ringed with stunning modern architecture, including César Pelli's **UniCredit Tower** and Michele de Lucchi's pod-like **UniCredit pavilion**, with Stefano Boeri's **Bosco Verticale** visible

across Studio Giorgetta's 'Library of Trees', a park inspired by botanic gardens.

## Fondazione Feltrinelli

ARCHITECTURE

3 ⊙ MAP P88, B4

Herzog & de Meuron's first public building in Italy is a combination of two elongated, slanted structures that look reminiscent of a greenhouse. That's no coincidence: they are built on the site of a former nursery and take inspiration from Milan's historic *cascine* (farmsteads). With a steeply pitched roof and shark-tooth edge, they bring an awesome dose of modernity to the surrounding neighbourhood. The foundation is also home to one of its namesake bookshops (open 8am to 11pm Monday to Friday, 9.30am to 11pm Saturday and Sunday) and an extremely good cafe. (☏02 495 83 41; www.fondazione feltrinelli.it; Viale Pasubio 5; ⊙9.30am-5.30pm Mon-Fri; Ⓜ Monumentale)

# Eating

## Casa Ramen Super

RAMEN $$

4 ✕ MAP P88, C1

Luca Catalfamo's second ramen restaurant really is super. Not least because you can book a seat here. His velvety-smooth ramen is still the highlight, but there are other not-to-be-missed dishes like the pork and fermented cabbage *gyoza* (dumplings) and the irresistible spicy ribs. Just remember to follow the 'Ramen Rules' and slurp up the last dregs of your soup noisily. (📞 02 8352 9210; www.casaramen super.com; Via Ugo Bassi 26; meals €15-35; 🕐12.30-3pm & 7.30-11.30pm Tue-Sat; ❄️✈️; Ⓜ️Isola)

## Berberè
PIZZA $

5 🍴 MAP P88, D2

Craft pizzas and craft beers is what Bolognese brothers Matteo and Salvatore promise you at this fantastically good pizzeria housed in an atmospheric 1950s cooperative. Everything from the Black Elk flour (they use variations of spelt, enkir and kamut, which give a lighter finish than wheat) to the Ponteré mozzarella, the Torre Guaceto tomatoes and Puglian *fiordilatte* (a semi-soft cheese) is sourced obsessively for the optimum flavour punch. Book ahead. (📞 02 3670 7820; www.berberepizza. it; Via Sebenico 21; pizza €6.50-14; 🕐7-11.30pm Mon-Fri, 12.30-2.30pm & 7-11.30pm Sat & Sun; Ⓜ️Isola)

## La Ravioleria Sarpi
CHINESE $

6 🍴 MAP P88, A4

This hole-in-the-wall Chinese takeaway has taken Milan by storm. It's a collaboration between a young Chinese economics student and one of the city's heritage DOC butchers, belonging to Walter Sirtori next door. The result is a range of plump, Jiaozi dumplings inspired by Agie's grandmother, which are stuffed with just three fillings: beef and leek, pork and cabbage or rough-chopped vegetables. (📞 331 8870596; Via Paolo

Sarpi 27; dumplings €3-5; 🕐10am-3pm & 4-9.30pm; ✈️; 🚊12, 14)

## Ratanà
MILANESE $$

7 🍴 MAP P88, D3

Located in a lovely Liberty building that once belonged to the railway, Cesare Battisti's neo-bistro turns out authentic Milanese flavours. Drawing his produce from Slow Food artisans, the menu offers up classics such as roasted pumpkin with *robiola* (soft cheese), risotto with turnip greens and crispy veal tongue with mash. There's a small bar, which locals mob at *aperitivo* (pre-dinner drink) time (6.30pm to 8pm). (📞 02 8712 8855; www. ratana.it; Via Gaetano de Castillia 28; meals €35-45; 🕐12.30-2.30pm & 7.30-11.30pm; Ⓜ️Gioia)

## Ristorante Berton
MODERN ITALIAN $$$

8 🍴 MAP P88, D4

Michelin-starred chef Andrea Berton is one of Milan's most decorated, and his namesake restaurant sits in a futuristic glass tower amid the skyscrapers of Porta Nuova. It's a fitting context for his light, contemporary cooking aiming to 'evolve' classic Lombard cuisine. Examples include ravioli made with rice to bump up the texture, or slow-cooked veal with lemons from Lago di Garda. (📞 02 6707 5801; www.ristoranteberton.com; Via Mike Bongiorno 13; meals €100-140; 🕐12.30-2.30pm & 8-10.30pm Tue-Fri, 7.30-10.30pm Mon & Sat; ❄️📶; Ⓜ️Repubblica)

## Antica Trattoria della Pesa

MILANESE $$$

9 ❌ MAP P88, B4

Recipe for instant nostalgia: take the landmark building where Ho Chi Minh stayed in the '30s, add literary types from nearby publishing houses, mix with comfort food – osso buco topped with gremolata, fillet steak with green peppercorns and *cotoletta* (crumbed veal cutlets) – spice it up with some red, and finish with a sigh over some smooth, boozy *zabaglione* (egg and Marsala custard). (📞02 655 57 41; www.anticatrattoriadellapesa.com; Viale Pasubio 10; meals €40-60; ⏱12.30-2.30pm & 7.30-11pm Mon-Sat; Ⓜ Garibaldi)

## 10 Corso Como Café

CAFE $$$

10 ❌ MAP P88, C4

A picture-perfect courtyard draped in greenery, and world-class people-watching awaits at Corso Como. Sit pretty in the black-and-white chairs and enjoy goblets of fruit smoothies, crisp vegetable crudités, grilled shrimp and the most stylish cheese sandwich you're ever likely to see. Plus it offers the ultimate afternoon tea: your choice of caviar and blinis (from €55) and a pot of Mariage Frères tea. (📞02 2901 3581; www.10corsocomo.it; Corso Como 10; meals €35-60; ⏱11am-1am; ❄; Ⓜ Garibaldi)

Cimitero Monumentale (p89)

## Food Galore at Eataly

There may not be a lot to see in this neighbourhood, but there is loads to eat, from some excellent traditional trattorias to good multi-cultural options and trendy bistros serving American-style brunches. At the centre of it all, on Piazza XXV Aprile, stands flagship Milanese foodstore **Eataly** (Map p88, C4; ☑02 4949 7301; www.eataly. net/it_it/negozi/milano-smeraldo; ⏰8.30am-midnight; 🛜♿; Ⓜ Moscova, Garibaldi), a cult destination dedicated to Italian gastronomy. Explore its four floors which are stocked with the best locally sourced products and 19 different eateries, including Michelin-starred restaurant, **Alice Ristorante** (☑02 4949 7340; www.aliceristorante.it; meals €110-130, lunch €50; ⏰12.30-2pm & 7.30-10pm Mon-Sat; ♨🍴), run by two of the most innovative female food talents in the city.

## Les Pommes   INTERNATIONAL $$

11 🍴 MAP P88, C2

Hankering for a burger made from Fassone beef or a smoked-salmon bagel? Then the menu at Les Pommes is for you. Diners can choose from Scandinavian, American, Mediterranean or Italian menus, which include plenty of fresh fruit and salads alongside the bagels, burgers and lobster rolls. Sunday brunch is packed with a young, cool crowd. Come early. (☑02 8707 4765; www.lespommes.it; Via Pastrengo 7; meals €18-30; ⏰8am-midnight Mon-Sun; Ⓜ Garibaldi)

# Drinking

## Cantine Isola   WINE BAR

12 🍷 MAP P88, A4

Only octogenarians make use of the table at the back – everyone else hovers near the beautiful old bar, balancing plates of bruschetta and holding glasses at the ready to sample wines from 400 exceptional vintners. The knowledgeable Sarais family, who own the bar, believe in the sharing the magic and offer many outstanding and rare wines by the glass. (www.cantineisola.com; Via Paolo Sarpi 30; ⏰10am-10pm Tue-Sun; 🚋12, 14)

## oTTo   CAFE

13 🍷 MAP P88, A4

How to define oTTo? It's a place to feel at home when you don't want to be at home (or in your hotel). Come here for breakfast; hang out with the co-workers and global nomads mid-morning; break for sociable lunches, cake-filled tea times and Aperol-fuelled *aperitivo*. The Danish-inspired smørrebrøds (open sandwiches) are healthy, there are movies and events. What's not to like? (www.sarpiotto.com; Via Paolo Sarpi 8; snacks €5-12; ⏰7pm-2am Mon, 10am-2am Tue-Sun; 🛜; Ⓜ Garibaldi FS)

## Ceresio 7 BAR

14 MAP P88, B3

Heady views match the heady price of *aperitivo* at Milan's coolest rooftop bar, sitting atop the former 1930s Enel (electricity company) HQ. Two pools, two bars and a restaurant under the guidance of former Bulgari head chef Elio Sironi make this a hit with Milan's beautiful people. In summer you can book a whole day by the pool from €110, which includes food and drinks. (www.ceresio7.com; Via Ceresio 7; aperitivo €18, meals €60-80; ⏱12.30pm-1am; 🛜; 🚋2, 4)

## Octavius Bar COCKTAIL BAR

15 MAP P88, C3

Despite its unpromising exterior in an intimidating, glassy skyscraper on Piazza Gae Aulenti, the Octavius surprises with its warm, glossy wooden interior and sexy, retro ambience reminiscent of a 1930s ocean liner. The custom-made cocktails are sophisticated, too. The Suite 200 mixes organic Yaguara cachaça with lime juice, Maraschino liqueur and a homemade shrub of mango, lime, figs and vinegar. (www.replaythestage.com; Piazza Gae Aulenti 4; cocktails €16-18; ⏱6pm-1am Mon-Sat; Ⓜ Garibaldi FS)

## Frida BAR

16 MAP P88, C2

The jumble of tables in the heated courtyard and the comfy couches inside make it easy to bond over beer or regional wine with an arty crowd. The *aperitivo* spread is continuously replenished and sports plenty of veg dishes. No pretensions, no entourages, just good music, good value and good times. (www.fridaisola.it; Via Pollaiuolo 3; ⏱noon-3pm & 6pm-2am Mon-Fri, 11.30am-2am Sat, 5pm-1am Sun; 🛜👫; Ⓜ Zara, Garibaldi)

## Botanical Club BAR

17 MAP P88, C2

This bar-bistro is Italy's first foray into microdistillery. Mixologist Katerina Logvinova has over 150 gins to play with, including the house brand, Spleen & Ideal, which experiments with interesting botanicals such as Serbian juniper and tonka beans. To accompany divine concoctions like Chinese Dusk (London Dry Gin, sake, plum bitters and fruit liqueur) are contemporary plates of veal tartare and crab salad. (www.thebotanicalclub.com; Via Pastrengo 11; meals €25-30; ⏱12.30-2.30pm & 6.30-10.30pm Mon-Fri, 6.30-10.30pm Sat; 🛜; Ⓜ Isola)

## Alcatraz CLUB

18 MAP P88, B1

Founded by Italian rock-star Vasco Rossi, Alcatraz is now a multifunctional venue for live concerts, DJ sets, fashion shows and a weekly dance club. The 3000-sq-metre former garage space rocks to the sound of Latino, house and revival on Fridays and classic rock 'n' roll on Saturday. (https://alcatraz

milano.it; Via Valtellina 25; tickets from €10; M Maciachini)

# Entertainment

## Blue Note JAZZ

19 ⭐ MAP P88, C1

Top-class jazz acts from around the world perform here at the only European outpost for New York's Blue Note jazz club. If you haven't prebooked, you can buy tickets at the door from 7.30pm. It also does a popular easy-listening Sunday brunch (€35 per adult, or €70 for two adults and two children under 12). (📞02 6901 6888; www.bluenotemilano. com; Via Borsieri 37; tickets €30-70; ⏰7.30pm-midnight Tue-Sun Sep-Jun; M Isola, Zara)

## La Fabbrica del Vapore PERFORMING ARTS

20 ⭐ MAP P88, A3

This industrial site once housed a factory for electric trams; now it lends its vast warehouses to a centre of the arts particularly aimed at developing the creative skills of young people. Dance, photography, theatre, cinema and concerts fill the factory's program year-round. (www.fabbricadelvapore.org; Via Procaccini 4; admission free; ♿; 🚋7, 12, 14)

# Shopping

## Claudio Calestani JEWELLERY, ACCESSORIES

21 🔒 MAP P88, C1

For the ultimate rock 'n' roll–biker look, drop into this renowned silver-

10 Corso Como Café (p91)

smith for a custom look wallet chain, a braided leather and silver bracelet and an iguana or calf-skin belt with a swirling silver buckle made using the lost-wax casting technique. The key chains, pocket knives and jewellery also make great gifts. (www.claudiocalestani.it; Via Thaon di Revel 3; ⏱11am-7pm Tue-Sat; Ⓜ Isola)

## 10 Corso Como
FASHION & ACCESSORIES

This might be the world's most hyped 'concept shop', but Carla Sozzani's selection of desirable things (Lanvin ballet flats, Alexander Girard wooden dolls, a demi-couture frock by a designer you've not read about *yet*) makes 10 Corso Como (see 10 🍴 Map p88, C4) a fun window-shopping experience. There's a bookshop upstairs with art and design titles, and a hyper-stylish bar and restaurant in the main atrium and picture-perfect courtyard. (www.10corsocomo.com; Corso Como 10; ⏱10.30am-7.30pm Fri-Tue, to 9pm Wed & Thu; Ⓜ Garibaldi)

## Zaini
CHOCOLATE

22 🔒 MAP P88, C3

In 1913 Luigi Zaini opened his first chocolate factory and this sweet-filled store is located where it once stood. Although you're welcome to wrap your chops around the unctuous hot chocolate laced with rosebuds served at the bar, the big seller here is 'Emilia', a dark-chocolate delight named after the nanny who

tested many of the recipes in the family kitchen. (www.zainimilano.com; Via de Cristoforis 5; ⏱7.30am-9.30pm Tue-Fri, to 8pm Mon, 9am-9.30pm Sat, 9am-7pm Sun; 👬; Ⓜ Garibaldi)

## Deus Ex Machina
SPORTS & OUTDOORS

23 🔒 MAP P88, C1

This massive outpost of the uber-cool Australian surf-and-biker brand is a testament to Isola's current *movida* (cool). Browse among the hand-built motorcycles and bikes, MAKR tool rolls, Carhartt threads and Bell helmets and try not to spend a fortune. Alternatively, just soak up the vibe at the in-house restaurant or out in the pink courtyard where those in-the-know refer for *aperitivo*. (http://deuscustoms.com/cafes/milan; Via Thaon di Revel 3; ⏱9.30am-1am Sun-Thu, to 2am Fri & Sat; 🛜; Ⓜ Isola)

## Ziio
JEWELLERY

24 🔒 MAP P88, D3

Elizabeth Paradon's unique handworked jewellery is coveted the world over by celebrities and fashionistas. Combining micro-Murano glass beads, gold, silver and semiprecious stones, pearls and coral, the bold and colourful creations are influenced by decorative motifs from Venice, Greece, Egypt and the Far East. (📞02 3670 6771; http://ziio.org; Via Gaetano di Castillia 20; ⏱10.30am-2.30pm & 3-7pm Mon-Sat; Ⓜ Garibaldi)

# Explore

# Corso Magenta & Sant'Ambrogio

*Leonardo da Vinci's The Last Supper (p98) and the Basilica di Sant'Ambrogio (p103) draw visitors to these leafy streets, but there's an equal mix of sacred and secular here. Milan's stock exchange sits on Piazza degli Affari (p103), hence the chic shops on Corso Magenta. To the south and west, the vibe grows more casual, influenced by students at the sprawling Università Cattolica.*

*A pastry at historic Marchesi (p105) marks the start of the day. Then, head to the Museo Nazionale Scienza e Tecnologia (p100) for a morning marvelling at models of Leonardo's war machines. Grab a gourmet panino at De Santis (p105) and toss a coin for your next stop: St Ambrogio's tomb at Milan's most important basilica, or Bernardino Luini's heavenly frescoes at the Chiesa di San Maurizio (p103). With your evening ticket for The Last Supper tucked safely in your pocket, stop for a leisurely glass of wine at Ricerca Vini (p106) or Bottiglieria Bulloni (p107) before hotfooting it to gaze on Leonardo da Vinci's masterful mural in the refectory of Basilica di Santa Maria delle Grazie (p103).*

## Getting There & Around

M For the Science Museum and the Basilica di Sant'Ambrogio take M2 (green line) and exit at Sant'Ambrogio; for Corso Magenta and *The Last Supper* you can exit either at Sant'Ambrogio or Cadorna, which is also served by M1 (red line).

🚊 Trams 16 and 27 run along Corso Magenta, while trams 2, 3 and 14 run down Via Torino and may be convenient for the Basilica di Sant'Ambrogio.

### Corso Magenta Map on p102

Chiesa di San Maurizio (p103) YURI TURKOV/SHUTTERSTOCK ©

## Top Experience 📷

# Admire Leonardo da Vinci's Last Supper

◉ MAP P102, C2

www.cenacolovinciano.net

Piazza Santa Maria delle Grazie 2

adult/reduced €12/7, plus booking fee €2

🕐 8.15am-6.45pm Tue-Sun

Ⓜ Cadorna

*Milan's most famous painting, Leonardo da Vinci's Last Supper, is hidden away on a wall of the refectory adjoining the Basilica di Santa Maria delle Grazie (pictured above). Depicting Christ and his disciples at the dramatic moment when Christ reveals he is aware of the betrayal afoot, it is a masterful psychological study and one of the world's most iconic images.*

# The Last Supper

*The Last Supper* is a landmark painting. Art historians identify it as the beginning of the High Renaissance, and it is unquestionably superior to all the efforts of even the greatest masters who came before. But it isn't just technique that sets the 42-sq-metre mural apart; even today it possesses a subtlety of tone, grace of line and vivid narrative power few images possess.

Twenty-two years of delicate restoration have stabilised the fragile image. Da Vinci himself was partly to blame: his experimental mix of oil and tempera was applied between 1495 and 1498, rather than within a week as is typical with fresco techniques. The Dominicans didn't help matters when in 1652 they raised the refectory floor, hacking off Jesus' feet. The most damage, however, was caused by restorers in the 19th century, whose use of alcohol and cotton wool removed an entire layer. But the work's condition does little to lessen its astonishing beauty.

## The 'Other' Fresco

At the other end of the refectory is Giovanni Donato da Montorfano's fresco of the *Crucifixion*. It was painted in 1495 at the same time as Leonardo was working on his masterpiece and there is even an iconographic relationship between the two: Christ's upturned left hand points towards Montorfano's 'good thief', while his right hand is turned downwards in the direction of the unrepentant thief. Still, you can't believe the two works are contemporaneous; unlike Leonardo's natural, lateral, free-flowing scene, Montorfano's image is structured and stiff: a dense throng of expressionless soldiers and saints amassed around the Cross, backed by a stilted image of Jerusalem with Christ rising above the fray, arms unnaturally held aloft. It seems like a work from another century.

## ★ Top Tips

o Reservations for *The Last Supper* must be made weeks in advance.

o At shorter notice you can take a €75 city tour with **Autostrada Viaggi** (☏02 3008 9900; www.autostradaleviaggi.it; Passaggio Duomo 2; tours €65-125; ☺9am-6pm Mon-Fri, to 4pm Sat & Sun; 🚻; Ⓜ Duomo), which guarantees a visit to the mural.

o Once booked, you'll be allotted a strict visiting time of 15 minutes between 8.15am and 6.45pm. Arrive early to pick up tickets and audio guides.

o Multilingual guided tours (€3.50) need to be reserved in advance.

## ✕ Take a Break

Grab a quick coffee or beer with locals at De Santis (p105).

Follow Leonardo's divine dining experience with a meal in the garden courtyard at La Brisa (p106).

## Top Experience 📸
# Explore the Museo Nazionale Scienza e Tecnologia

*Would-be inventors will go goggle-eyed at Milan's Museo Nazionale Scienza e Tecnologia Leonardo da Vinci, the largest science museum in Italy. It is a fitting tribute in a city where the arch inventor did much of his finest work. The 16th-century monastery that houses the museum features a collection of more than 10,000 items, including steam trains, planes and full-sized galleons.*

◎ MAP P102, C3

www.museoscienza.org

Via San Vittore 21

adult/child €10/7.50, submarine tours €8, flight simulator €8

🕑 9.30am-5pm Tue-Fri, to 6.30pm Sat & Sun

Ⓜ Sant'Ambrogio

# Leonardo da Vinci Gallery

In 1481, Leonardo da Vinci wrote to Ludovico Sforza applying for a position at court. He had been recommended as a musician but he promoted himself as an engineer, promising the duke he could build him all manner of war machines, improve the castle fortifications and tinker with the canal system; plus, if there was nothing else to do, he could always paint. He filled dozens of notebooks with sketches that have now been realised here in the world's largest collection of da Vinci models, in order to better understand his revolutionary ideas.

# Transport Pavilions

One of the museum's biggest draws are the huge transport pavilions filled with steam trains, ships, and planes suspended from the rafters. Exquisitely crafted 18th- and 19th-century models (including Enrico Forlanini's 1877 experimental helicopter) sit beside the real thing. Highlights include the 1921 brigantine schooner *Ebe*, the Macchi MC205 Veltro fighter plane and the *Enrico Toti* submarine, for which you need to book a guided tour.

# Space Exhibit

Housed in a gallery curated by the president of the Italian Space Society, this display holds some real treasures, not least the amazing 17th-century celestial and terrestrial globes by Coronelli and Moroncelli, Giovanni Schiaparelli's Merz-Repsold telescope that gave rise to the myth of Martians, and a moon rock from the Apollo 17 voyage.

## ★ Top Tips

o Give yourself at least half a day to explore the 50,000-sq-metre museum.

o The museum has an extensive program of interactive laboratories for children in English and Italian.

o You can only board the *Enrico Toti* submarine on a tour (€10), which should be booked at the ticket desk in advance.

o The museum's **MUST Shop** (02 4855 5340; www.mustshop.it; Via Olona 6; 10am-7pm Tue-Sun; M Sant'Ambrogio) sells all manner of science-inspired books, design items, gadgets and games.

## ✗ Take a Break

Stop for coffee or a tasty homemade *panini* (sandwich) at Bar Anny (p106).

After working up a hunger, head to Osteria la Carbonaia (p105) for a hefty grilled steak.

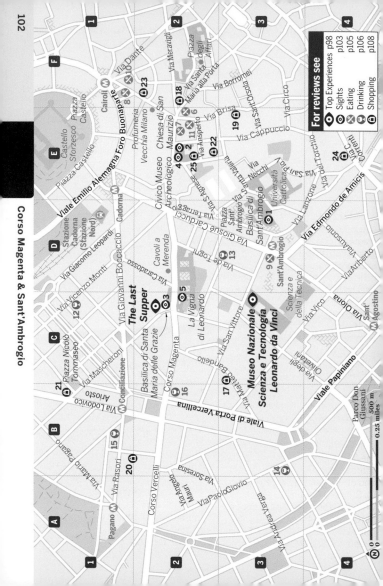

# Corso Magenta & Sant'Ambrogio

For reviews see
- Top Experiences p98
- Sights p103
- Eating p105
- Drinking p106
- Shopping p108

The Last Supper

Museo Nazionale Scienza e Tecnologia Leonardo da Vinci

# Sights

## Basilica di Sant'Ambrogio

BASILICA

### 1 ⊙ MAP P102, D3

St Ambrose, Milan's patron saint and one-time superstar bishop, is buried in the crypt of this red-brick cathedral, which he founded in 379 CE. It's a fitting legacy, built and rebuilt with a purposeful simplicity that is truly uplifting: the seminal Lombard Romanesque basilica. Shimmering altar mosaics and a biographical golden altarpiece (835), which once served as the cladding for the saint's sarcophagus, light up the shadowy vaulted interior. (www.basilicasantambrogio.it; Piazza Sant'Ambrogio 15; admission free; ⊙10am-noon & 2.30-6pm Mon-Sat, 3-5pm Sun; MSant'Ambrogio)

## Chiesa di San Maurizio

CHURCH

### 2 ⊙ MAP P102, E2

This 16th-century royal chapel and one-time Benedictine convent is Milan's hidden crown jewel, every inch of it covered in breathtaking frescoes, most of them executed by Bernardino Luini, who worked with Leonardo da Vinci. Many of the frescoes immortalise Ippolita Sforza, Milanese literary maven, and other members of the powerful Sforza and Bentivoglio clans who paid for the chapel's decoration. (⊋02 8844 5208; Corso Magenta 15; admission free; ⊙9.30am-7.30pm Tue-Sun; MCadorna)

## Basilica di Santa Maria delle Grazie

BASILICA

### 3 ⊙ MAP P102, C2

Begun by Guiniforte Solari in 1463, with later additions by Bramante, this handsome Lombard church encapsulates the magnificence of the Milanese court of Ludovico Sforza and Beatrice d'Este. Articulated in fine brickwork and terracotta, the building is robust but fanciful; its apse is topped by a masterful, drum-shaped dome and its interior is lined with frescoed chapels decorated by the likes of Bernardo Zenale, Antonello da Messina and Bramantino. (www.legraziemilano.it; Piazza Santa Maria delle Grazie; admission free; ⊙7am-12.55pm & 3-5.55pm Mon-Sat, 3.30pm-5.55pm Sun; MCadorna, ⊟16)

### Piazza degli Affari

Home to the Italian stock exchange, this **piazza** (Map p102; MCordusio) is a famous hub of financial activity. But that's not all it's known for. In the centre of the piazza is Milan's most controversial public sculpture, Maurizio Cattelan's **L.O.V.E.** (standing for 'Liberty, Hatred, Vendetta and Eternity'). A 4m-high fist with a raised middle finger, many believe it's a statement on the economic crisis as it was erected just after the financial crash, although the artist has refrained from commenting.

## Civico Museo Archeologico

MUSEUM

4 ⊙ MAP P102, E2

The 8th-century Monastero Maggiore, once the most important Benedictine convent in the city, is now home to Milan's archaeological museum. Access is via a cloister, where fragments of the city's Roman walls can be seen. Ground-floor rooms display important artefacts from Roman Mediolanum, while on upper floors the city's history unfolds in well-curated collections of Etruscan, Greek, Gothic and Lombard artefacts. In the garden, the 3rd-century frescoed **Ansperto Tower** marks the limits of Mediolanum's city walls. (www.museoarcheologicomilano.it; Corso Magenta 15; adult/child €5/3; ⊙9am-5.30pm Tue-Sun; Ⓜ Cadorna)

## La Vigna di Leonardo

HISTORIC SITE

5 ⊙ MAP P102, C2

Behind the 15th-century Casa degli Atellani, lies one of the most interesting gardens in Milan. Set within them are the original vines of Leonardo da Vinci, who was gifted the land by Ludovico Sforza in return for his work on *The Last Supper*. Leonardo cherished the vineyard and the tour of the garden and *palazzo* (mansion), gives a unique insight into the deeply layered history of the city. (www.vignadileonardo.com; Corso Magenta 65; adult/reduced €10/8; ⊙9am-6pm; 🚊16, 19)

Basilica di Sant'Ambrogio (p103)

# Eating

## Pasticceria Marchesi  PASTRIES $

6 MAP P102, E2

This wood-panelled *pasticceria* (pastry shop) has been baking since 1824 and turns out 10 different types of brioche alongside *bignes* (cream puffs), millefeuilles, pralines and more. The window displays have the feel of a Hitchcock dream sequence but, with perfect-every-shot coffee, there's no shock ending. (02 86 27 70; www.pasticceriamarchesi.it; Via Santa Maria alla Porta 11/a; 7.30am-8pm Mon-Sat, 8.30am-1pm Sun; Cairoli, Cordusio)

## De Santis  SANDWICHES $

7 MAP P102, E2

Sandwiches here are so damn good you may eschew restaurant dining just to sample that *panini* with prosciutto, spicy goat cheese, pepperoni, aubergine and artichokes. There are 200 variations on the menu and De Santis' decades of experience are good reasons why punters are prepared to queue at this tiny venue. Beer is served on tap to the lucky few who find seating. (02 7209 5124; www.paninide santis.it; Corso Magenta 9; sandwiches €6-8; noon-11.30pm Sun-Thu, to 12.30am Fri & Sat; ; Cadorna)

## Da Rita e Antonio  PIZZA $

8 MAP P102, F1

Serving the neighbourhood since 1972, this restaurant continues to

### Cavoli a Merenda

Join Vanessa and Carlo in their aristocratic **palazzo** (Map p102, D2; 338 4679513; www.cavoliamerenda.eu; Corso Magenta 66; lessons €65-80; 7.30-10.30pm Mon-Fri; 16, 19) where you'll learn the secrets of preparing perfect Italian dishes. Vanessa has a background in nutrition while Carlo is an affable host with a stream of fascinating travel stories. After the lesson, the group sits down to eat the meal prepared on the pretty flower-ringed terrace.

do exactly what it's always done: soft, fluffy Neapolitan pizza with a raised rim that tenderly cradles toppings of gooey mozzarella from Prati del Volturno dairy, spicy salami and anchovies with Sicilian capers. Other dishes such as homemade gnocchi feature on the menu, but why mess with a perfect recipe? (02 87 55 79; www.daritae antonio.it; Via Giacomo Puccini 2; pizza €6.50-9; noon-3pm & 7pm-midnight Tue-Fri & Sun, 6pm-midnight Sat; Cairoli)

## Osteria la Carbonaia  GRILL $$

9 MAP P102, D3

This homespun trattoria is famous for its meat dishes, particularly the velvety *tagliata* (sliced beef) served with grilled vegetables and roasted potatoes. The brick-lined grill station – which turns out ribs, sausages and glorious Fiorentina steaks – sits centre stage, and the low, beamed ceiling and colourful picture-lined walls give the place a comfortable, homely atmosphere. (📞02 4800 0088; www.osterialacarbonaia.it; Via Carducci 38; meals €40-45; ⏱12.30-2.30pm & 7.30-11pm Mon-Fri, 7.30-11pm Sat; Ⓜ Sant'Ambrogio)

## Cucina del Toro   MILANESE $$

10 ❌ MAP P102, F1

A solid favourite of the lunching business crowd, this elegant *osteria* (tavern) offers a short menu of classic dishes with the focus on quality ingredients. Beef *carnesalada* (salt-cured meat) from Trentino is followed by lemon or saffron risotto and maybe braised tripe or roast pork. Ask for advice on the well-priced wines, and don't miss the cheese plate. (📞02 87 51 07; www.cucinadeltoro. it; Via Manfredo Camperio 15; meals €40-50; ⏱12.30-2.30pm & 7.30-10.30pm Mon-Fri, 7.30-10.30pm Sat; ❄; Ⓜ Cairoli)

## La Brisa   MODERN ITALIAN $$$

11 ❌ MAP P102, E2

Discreet, elegant and exquisitely romantic. Push open the screened door and the maître d' will guide you to a table beneath centuries-old linden trees in a secluded courtyard, where ivy climbs the walls and pink hydrangeas bob in the breeze. Chef Antonio Facciolo's seasonal menus are similarly elegant; his signature dish is a mouth-watering roast pork in a myrtle-berry drizzle. (📞02 8645 0521; www.ristorantelabrisa.it; Via Brisa 15; meals €50-70; ⏱12.45-2.30pm & 7.45-10.30pm Mon-Fri, 7.45-10.30pm Sun; ❄; Ⓜ Cairoli, Cordusio)

# Drinking

## Ricerca Vini   WINE BAR

12 🍷 MAP P102, C1

Sure, it's a wine shop, but it's a bar and a rather good restaurant, too. What better place to sample your options before committing to carry home one of the 2500 wines on offer here. It's one of the largest selections in the city, and the *aperitivo* platters of prosciutto and cheese are excellent. Some evenings it hosts tastings. (www. ricercavini.it; Via Vicenzo Monti 33; ⏱10am-1pm & 3.30-10pm Tue-Sat, 4-10pm Mon; Ⓜ Cadorna)

## Bar Anny   CAFE

13 🍷 MAP P102, D3

Tucked down a quiet street with its grand villas is this retro '70s bar with its friendly proprietor, Antonio. Drop by for a chat and a cappuccino in the wood-panelled bar or take a seat in the tiny galleried dining area and order one (or three) of its famous homemade sandwiches stuffed full of hearty Lombard cheeses and hand-cut prosciutto. (Via Aristide de Togni 15; sandwiches €4.50; ⏱7am-1am Mon-Sat; Ⓜ Sant'Ambrogio)

## Bottiglieria Bulloni      WINE BAR

14 ⓜ MAP P102, B3

Selling liquor and wine since 1933, this *bottiglieria* (liquor store) is the real deal when it comes to *aperitivo* time. Here it's strictly crostini, olives and gherkins, and a well-executed €6 *spritz*. Less than a dozen tables sit beneath the bottle-lined walls (glasses of wine €4 to €8), and behind the bar there's an original futurist artwork by Enrico Prampolini. (www.bottiglieriabulloni.it; Via Lipari 2; ⏰7am-10.30pm Mon-Sat; Ⓜ Sant'Agostino)

## Rufus Cocktail Bar      COCKTAIL BAR

15 ⓜ MAP P102, B1

This neighbourhood bar fills a critical gap by supplying some good grown-up cocktails to the thirsty punters on Corso Vercelli. Although it serves breakfast, it's at *aperitivo* time that the warm brick interior and chandelier-heavy bar shines. Drinks range from the traditional Campari to the contemporary Cup of Life with lime, bitters, gin and soda. (www.rufuscocktailbar.com; Via Alberto da Giussano 2; ⏰7.30am-1.30pm & 5.30pm-1am Mon-Sat; 🛜; Ⓜ Conciliazione)

## Biffi Pasticceria      CAFE

16 ⓜ MAP P102, B2

Proud keepers of a traditional *panetùn* (panettone) sweet bread recipe that once pleased Pope Pius X, Biffi has changed little since its 1847 opening. With its polished walnut bar and Murano chandeliers, its air of old-world elegance continues to attract

De Santis (p105)

the good people of Milan, who come to meet over dainty cream cakes, coffee and cocktails. (📞02 4800 6702; www.biffipasticceria.it; Corso Magenta 87; ⏰6am-9pm; 👬; Ⓜ Conciliazione)

# Shopping

## Spazio Rossana Orlandi    DESIGN

17 🔒 MAP P102, C3

Installed in a former tie factory in the Magenta district, its iconic interior design studio is a challenge to find. Once inside, though, it's hard to leave the dream-like treasure trove stacked with vintage and contemporary limited-edition furniture, light fixtures, rugs and highly desirable homeware accessories from young and upcoming artists. (www.rossanaorlandi.com; Via Bandello 14; ⏰10am-7pm Mon-Sat; Ⓜ Sant'Ambrogio)

## Taschen    BOOKS

18 🔒 MAP P102, F2

Despite Taschen's catalogue of beautiful books, it's the interior of their Via Meravigli showroom that steals the show. Art books sit splendidly in steel cabinets and on a canary yellow, Corian-topped island, while underfoot Jonas Wood's terrazzo floors depict super-sized flowers and foliage. Take Salvatore Licitra's multi-coloured staircase upstairs for a selection of art prints and the latest collectable editions. (www.taschen.com; Via Meravigli 17; ⏰10am-7pm; Ⓜ Cairoli)

## Pellini    JEWELLERY

19 🔒 MAP P102, E3

Pellini's original 1947 atelier and archive is a beautiful galleried space with parquet floors, granite pillars and vintage wooden cabinets. Dotted around the gallery on tables, mannequins and in cabinets are Donatella's iridescent resin bangles and pendants, alongside drop earrings and long necklaces in colourful semi-precious stones, glass, crystal and steel. Everything is handmade. (www.pellini.it; Via Morigi 9; ⏰9.30am-7.30pm Mon-Fri; 🚌16, 19)

## Al Bazar    FASHION & ACCESSORIES

20 🔒 MAP P102, B1

Created by Milanese fashion icon Lino Ieluzzi, this store is a must for all sartorially inclined men. More than just showcasing the Italian look, it's about capturing the Lino look. Think double-breasted suits, wide lapels and big bold colours. Everything is top quality (of course) and has to some extent been designed by the man himself. (www.albazarmilano.it; Via Scarpa 9; ⏰8.30am-7pm Mon-Sat; Ⓜ Pagano)

## Pupi Solari    CHILDREN'S CLOTHING

21 🔒 MAP P102, B1

Many Milanese from a certain kind of family will recall regular Pupi Solari visits for shoe fittings and picking out exquisitely decorated party dresses or tweed jackets just like daddy's. This flagship store, opened in 1978 and still presided over by 89-year-old fashion doyenne

Pupi, continues to set the tone for Milan's aspiring middle class. (www.pupisolari.it; Piazza Tommaseo 2; ☺3-7pm Mon, from 10am Tue-Sat; 🚻; Ⓜ Conciliazione, 🚋29, 30)

## Galleria L'Affiche ART

22 🔒 MAP P102, E2

A treasure trove of vintage posters, fine-art prints, playbills and photographs, Galleria L'Affiche has a cult following and loyal stable of artists who entrust it with some of their finest work. Invest a few euros in some kitsch vintage postcards or spend several hundreds on a collectable; either way, you'll have hours of fun here. (www.affiche.it; Via Nirone 11; ☺2.30-8pm Mon, from 10am Tue-Sat; 🚋16)

## Risi FASHION & ACCESSORIES

23 🔒 MAP P102, F2

Head to Risi for a dose of effortless Milanese chic. Here you can stock up on soft grey and white linen shirts and trousers; honeycomb polo shirts in sober colours; and comfortable beachwear in classic pinstripes. Season-appropriate weights and wefts and an absence of logos mean you'll blend in with the natives. (www.risimilano.com; Via San Giovanni sul Muro 21; ☺3-7.30pm Mon, 10am-2.30pm & 3-7.30pm Tue-Sat; Ⓜ Cairoli)

## Atelier VM JEWELLERY

24 🔒 MAP P102, E4

It's easy to miss this hidden gem at the end of Via Correnti, despite

### A Piece of Shopping History 🛍️

Those dashing about town between sights and fashion shows may miss **Profumeria Vecchia Milano** (Map p102, E2; Via San Giovanni sul Muro 8; ☺9am-7pm Mon-Sat; Ⓜ Cairoli), which is an architectural slice of life from 19th-century Milan. Exclusive perfumes and creams are stocked in glass-fronted mahogany cabinets with gilded details all the way from the floral floor tiles to the stuccoed ceilings. Insider's tip: massages are available in the treatment rooms out back.

the neon sign. Founded by local designers Marta Caffarelli and Viola Naj Oleari, the shop is discreet, cool and elegant, a perfect match for the delicate, romantic pieces of jewellery. (www.ateliervm.com; Via Correnti 26; ☺3-7pm Mon, 10am-2pm & 3-7pm Tue-Sat; 🚋2, 14)

## Amelia CHILDREN'S CLOTHING

25 🔒 MAP P102, E2

Amelia's kidswear collection is a triumph of restrained style, mixing ruffles, rhinestones and hand-stitched detailing with simple shapes and the softest natural fabrics. Traditional toys and the cutest line of shoes will ensure your little darling is an ambassador of good taste. (www.ameliamilano.it; Via Nirone 10; ☺3-7pm Mon, 10am-2pm & 3-7pm Tue-Sat; 🚻; 🚋16, 19)

# Explore

# Navigli

*Named after its most identifiable feature – the canals, which once powered the city's fortunes – Navigli is now better known for its boutiques, bars and nightlife. Remnants of the city's ancient past, such as the Roman basilica of San Lorenzo, the early-Christian church of Sant'Eustorgio and the 19th-century triumphal arch on Piazza XXIV Maggio, provide a picturesque backdrop to the scene.*

*Start the day among relics of Roman Milan on Corsa di Porta Ticinese, where you can wander around the basilicas of San Lorenzo (p115) and Sant'Eustorgio (p115). Then head south to the old dock. In summer, you can jump aboard a boat and cruise out of Milan, or otherwise just enjoy the canalside window-shopping. Then head across the rail tracks at Porta Genova into Zona Tortona. Once a working-class neighbourhood, Tortona is now flush with design HQs and contemporary museums, hosting interesting international exhibitions. Circle back to the canals in the early evening for aperitivo (predinner drinks and/or snacks). The bars here are some of the best in the city.*

## Getting There & Around

Ⓜ Porta Genova on M2 (green line) is the closest stop for the canals; Sant'Agostino, also on M2, is convenient for Parco Solari and Viale Papiniano.

🚊 Use tram 3 for the shops along Corso di Porta Ticinese, Piazza XXIV Maggio and the Alzaia Naviglio Pavese canal; tram 9 travels east to west down Viale Col di Lana and Via Vigevano.

Navigli Map on p114

Basilica di San Lorenzo (p115) GEORGIOS TSICHLIS/SHUTTERSTOCK ©

# Walking Tour 🚶

## Life on the Canals

*Ever since the Renaissance the warehouses and factories lining Milan's canals have been a hive of creative and commercial endeavour. Locals love the area for weekend shopping and canalside drinking and dining. Post Expo, the area looks better than ever with revamped pedestrian walkways, new cycle paths and the restored centrepiece, the historic dock.*

### Walk Facts

**Start** Piazzale di Porta Lodovico 2; 🚋 3, 9

**End** Via Giosuè Borsi 9; 🚋 3

**Length** 4km; six hours

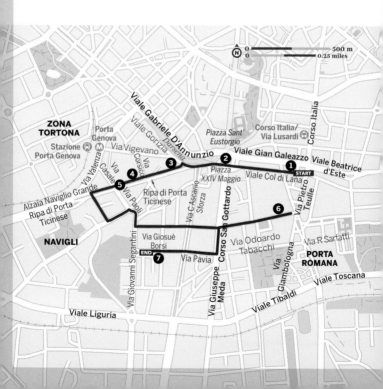

## ❶ Breakfast at Gattullo

Rise early to get the best of the bountiful pastry bar at **Gattullo** (☎02 5831 0497; www.gattullo.it; Piazzale di Porta Lodovico 2; pastries from €1.50; ⏰7am-9pm Tue-Sun; ❄; 🚊3, 9) before locals devour all the myrtle-berry croissants and delicate *sfogliatelle* (sweetened ricotta pastries) stuffed with divine Chantilly cream.

## ❷ Hanging Out at the Darsena

Milan's *darsena* (dock) was once the city's main port. It has now been transformed into a pedestrian piazza with a dockside **food market** (Piazza XXIV Maggio; ⏰8.30am-1pm & 4-7.30pm Tue-Sat, 8.30am-1pm Mon; 🚊3, 9) and a grassy park. Hunt down Giuseppe Zen's artisanal bread, meat and cheese stalls for a tasty mid-morning snack.

## ❸ Boat Tours

Canals were the autostradas of medieval Milan. The largest of them, the Naviglio Grande, was one of the city's busiest thoroughfares in the late 13th century. From April to September you can take a boat tour along it with **Navigli Lombardi** (☎02 3008 9940; www.naviglilombardi.it; Alzaia Naviglio Grande 4; adult/reduced €14/10; ⏰Apr-Sep; Ⓜ Porta Genova, 🚊3) .

## ❹ Neighbourhood Market

On the last Sunday of the month the **Mercatone dell'Antiquariato** (www.navigliogra, Genova, 🚊9) sets up along the Naviglio Grande. With more than 400 well-vetted antique traders, it provides hours of treasure-hunting pleasure.

## ❺ Window Browsing

Navigli is home to a thriving community of artists and musicians. Their eclectic studios line the canals. Join locals browsing the length of the Naviglio Grande for classic vinyl, artful comics and vintage radios.

## ❻ Aperitivo Hour

Almost every bar along Naviglio Grande offers an *aperitivo* buffet, but locals swear by the top scene at the converted metal foundry, **Fonderie Milanesi** (☎02 3652 7913; www.fonderiemilanesi.it; Via Giovenale 7; aperitivo €8; ⏰7pm-2am Tue-Fri, 12.30-3pm & 7pm-1am Sat & Sun; 🚊9, 15).

## ❼ The Local Movida

Much like Paris' Left Bank or London's Soho, Navigli is the hub of Milan's *movida* (nightlife) scene. Nowhere is cooler than **Apollo Club** (☎02 3826 0176; www.apollomilano.com; Via Giosuè Borsi 9; cocktails €8-10, meals €33-77; ⏰7pm-3am Wed-Thu, to 4am Fri & Sat, noon-1am Sun; 🚊3), with its vintage-style bar and Friday Rollover dance night. Check out its Facebook page for up-to-date events.

Navigli

N
0 ___ 500 m
0 ___ 0.25 miles

Via Necchi
Via Brisa
Via Lanzone
Via Torino
Via della Palla
Via Olmetto
Via S Vito
Via Urbano III
Largo Carrobbio
Via Dis ciplini
Via C Correnti
20
21
Via Camminadella
Via Edmondo de Amicis
Via Vico
Piazza Sant'Agostino
Via Sant'Agostino
Via Olona
Via Ausonio
Via Arberto
Via Torti
Basilica di San Lorenzo
Parco delle Basiliche
Via Cesare da Sesto
Via Genova
10
56
3
Sant'Agostino
Piazza Vetra
13
Via Molino delle Armi
Parco Don Giussani
Viale Papiniano
Corso Genova
Via Marco d'Oggiono
Via Gaudenzio Ferrari
24
Corso di Porta Ticinese
Via Arena
Via Vetere
Via Cosimo del Fante
6
Ansaldo Workshops (250m)
ZONA TORTONA
Corso C Colombo
Viale Gabriele D'Annunzio
Darsena
23
7
Basilica di Sant'Eustorgio
Corso Italia
9
Viale Gorizia
Piazza Sant'Eustorgio
2
Via Sambuco
Via Marco Burigozzo
3
1
Stazione Porta Genova
Porta Genova
Via Vigevano
8
Via Corsico
Naviglio Grande
Macelleria Popolare
(R)esistenza Casearia
Piazza XXIV Maggio
Viale Gian Galeazzo
22
Viale Col di Lana
12
17
Via Valenza
Via Casale
Alzaia Naviglio Grande
16
4
Ripa di Porta Ticinese
15
Via Magolfa
Naviglio Pavese
Naviglio Grande
Via C Ascanio Sforza
Corso San Gottardo
Via Custodi
Via Pietro Teulié
14
Via Angelo Fumagalli
Via Paoli
NAVIGLI
19
Via Gola
Via Giovenale
Via Giambologna
Via Castelbarco
Via Giosuè Borsi
Via Pavia
Via Odoardo Tabacchi
18
Via Giovanni Segantini
Via Darwin
Alzaia Naviglio Pavese
Via Conchetta
Via Brioschi
Via Zamenhof
Romolo
Milano Romolo
Via La Spezia
Viale Liguria
11
Via Giuseppe Meda
Viale Tibaldi
Via Imperia

For reviews see
◉ Sights p115
✗ Eating p116
🄟 Drinking p118
★ Entertainment p119
🄐 Shopping p120

# Sights

## Museo delle Culture MUSEUM

1 ⊙ MAP P114, A3

Aiming to be a place of dialogue
between people and world
cultures, Milan's Museum of
Culture, housed in the ex-Ansaldo
factory, has an ambitious remit.
The huge industrial complex was
re-engineered by British architect
David Chipperfield into a series of
severe spaces in translucent glass
and concrete. Past shows have
included an exhibition of Jean-
Michel Basquiat's work focusing
on race and identity politics, and
world-class Frida Kahlo set in the
context of the museum's indigenous Mesoamerican artefacts
that informed her visual aesthetic.
(MUDEC; ☑02 5 49 17; www.mudec.
it; Via Tortona 56; exhibitions adult/
reduced €13/11; ☺2.30-7.30pm Mon,
9.30am-7.30pm Tue-Wed, Fri & Sun,
to 10.30pm Thu & Sat; P; Ⓜ Porta
Genova)

## Basilica di Sant'Eustorgio BASILICA

2 ⊙ MAP P114, C3

Built in the 4th century to house
the bones of the Three Kings,
Sant'Eustorgio is one of Milan's
oldest churches. Its harmonious
exterior belies its rabble-rousing
past as Milan's Inquisition HQ, but
the real draw is Pigello Portinari's
**chapel**. Representative of the
Medici bank in Milan, Portinari had
the cash to splash on Milan's finest

Renaissance chapel, frescoed with
masterpieces by Vicenzo Foppa.
(☑02 8940 2671; www.santeustorgio.
it; Piazza Sant'Eustorgio 3; chapel adult/
reduced €6/4; ☺10am-6pm; �🚋3, 9)

## Basilica di San Lorenzo BASILICA

3 ⊙ MAP P114, C2

It's difficult not to be bowled over
by this oft-ignored hotchpotch of
towers, lodges, apses and domes.
In spite of appearances, it really is
the one basilica. At its centre is an
early-Christian circular structure
with three adjoining octagonal
chapels, dating to the 4th century.
What's left of a Romanesque atrium
leads to the heart of the church and
before it stand 16 Roman columns,
now a hang-out for kissing teens.
(☑02 8940 4129; www.sanlorenzomag
giore.com; Corso di Porta Ticinese 39;
admission free; ☺8am-6.30pm Mon-
Sat, 9am-7pm Sun; �🚋3, 14)

### Inside La Scala

To glimpse the inner workings
of La Scala, visit the **Ansaldo
Workshops** (☑02 4335 3521;
www.teatroallascala.org; Via
Bergognone 34; per person €10;
☺9am-noon & 2-4pm Tue &
Thu; Ⓜ Porta Genova), where
the stage sets are crafted
and painted, and some 800
to 1000 new costumes are
handmade each season. Tours
must be booked in advance.

# Eating

## LatteNeve

GELATO $

4 🍴 MAP P114, B3

This award-winning gelateria focuses on organic ingredients such as yoghurt from the alpine region of Valtellina, Bronte pistachios from Sicily and IGP hazelnuts from Piedmont, which can be topped with a delicious housemade whipped cream. Vegan options include dairy-free dark chocolate and gluten-free cones are available. (Via Vigevano 27; cones & tubs €2.50-4.50; ⏱1-10pm Tue-Thu, to 11pm Fri-Sun; Ⓜ Porta Genova)

## Pasticceria Cucchi

PASTRIES $

5 🍴 MAP P114, C2

Little has changed at this historic Milanese *pasticceria* (pastry shop) founded in 1936. Its interior brims with old-world charm; waiters wear formal attire; and Signor Cucchi still patiently works the cash register. Attracting a mixed crowd of *sciure* (posh Milanese women), fashionable types and tourists, it's a great spot to sit and people-watch while indulging in sweet treats. (www.pasticceriacucchi.it; Corso Genova 1; pastries €1.50-3; ⏱7am-10pm Tue-Sun; Ⓜ Sant'Ambrogio)

## Gino Sorbillo

PIZZA $

6 🍴 MAP P114, A3

The king of Neapolitan pizza has taken Milan by storm with his organic, slow-levitation dough and divinely simple toppings of tomato, mozzarella, basil, broccoli, sweet peppers, spicy *'nduja* (salami) and Norcia ham. To reach perfection, the hand-kneaded dough is rested in wooden boxes first before being artfully twirled and baked in a giant wood-fired. (📞02 5810 4789; Via Montevideo 4; pizza €8-12; ⏱noon-3pm & 7-11pm; Ⓜ Porta Genova)

## Sixième Bistrò

BISTRO $$

7 🍴 MAP P114, C3

If you like your antipasti with a side of design then check out sultry Sixième, part of the Six Gallery complex which includes a vintage furniture gallery and a florist set around a courtyard. Inside, diners slouch on velvet cushions, sip sophisticated cocktails and nibble hangar steaks and homemade pasta beneath Isamu Noguchi lamps. (📞02 3651 9910; www.facebook.com/SixiemeBistro; Via Scaldasole 7; meals €30-60; ⏱noon-3pm & 7pm-midnight Mon-Sat; 🚌3)

## Taglio

ITALIAN $$

8 🍴 MAP P114, B3

A restaurant, deli, cafe and bar: Taglio pulls it all off with aplomb. Only high-quality ingredients are used, and a seasonal menu puts a spin on classic Italian dishes. It also takes its coffee seriously, rotating in small-batch roasts from around the world and serving them in contemporary styles – such as Chemex filters – that are rare in Milan. (📞02 3653 4294; www.taglio.me; Via Vigevano 10; meals €25-38; ⏱11am-3.30pm & 6pm-midnight Mon-Fri, 9am-midnight Sat & Sun; 🚌10)

## Osteria del Binari    ITALIAN $$

9 ⊗ MAP P114, A3

Crashing an Italian wedding is the only other way you'd come by such heaping platters of handmade pasta, select cuts of meat and home-baked pastries. With Tuscan wine and loved ones gathered around, someone's bound to feel a toast coming on. A big bonus in summer are the large garden and conservatories out back. (📞02 8940 6753; www.osteriadelbinari.com; Via Tortona 1; meals €35-45; ⊙noon-3.30pm & 7.30pm-2am; Ⓜ Porta Genova)

## Tokuyoshi    FUSION $$$

10 ⊗ MAP P114, B2

Take a creative culinary voyage from Japan to Italy with Yoji Tokuyoshi at the helm. One-time sous-chef of world renowned Osteria Francescana, this talented chef has already received a Michelin star for his efforts. Expect the unexpected, such as Parmesan tiramisu or cod-filled Sicilian *cannoli* (pastry shells). (📞02 8425 4626; www.ristorante tokuyoshi.com; Via San Calocero 3; meals €50-75; tasting menu €100-140; ⊙7-10.30pm Tue-Sat, 12.30-2.30pm & 7-10.30pm Sun; 🚋2, 14)

## Carlo e Camilla in Segheria    ITALIAN $$$

11 ⊗ MAP P114, C6

A 1930s sawmill has been repurposed to grand effect. With chandeliers and shimmering light, it creates a theatrical ambience for modern Italian cuisine by Michelin-star chef Carlo Cracco. The dishes

Carlo e Camilla in Segheria

## Street Food Favourites

Street food guru, Giuseppe Zen, is wowing Milanese with his locavore food stalls within the Mercato Comunale. Featuring bread, meat and cheese, the stalls not only sell top-quality produce but prepare tasty snacks to eat on the spot with glasses of superior local wine. Drop by for lunch and you'll eat some of the best food in Milan.

**Macelleria Popolare** (Map p114, C3; ☎ 02 3946 8368; www.mangiarid istrada.com; Piazza XXIV Maggio; panini €5-8, snacks €2.50-9; ⊙ 9am-10pm Tue-Thu, to midnight Fri-Sun; 🚋 9) This 'Popular Butcher' emphasises Italian specialities such as *lampredotto* (cow stomach) and *mondeghili* (Milanese meatballs).

**(R)esistenza Casearia** (Mercato Comunale; Map p114, C3; Piazza XXIV Maggio; cheese boards €10-25; ⊙ 9am-10pm Tue-Thu, to midnight Fri-Sun; 🚋 9) Serves some of the finest raw-milk cheeses in Lombardy, all of which come from heritage producers who graze their animals on high-mountain pastures. Make a meal of it with the housemade tiramisu featuring the most creamy mascarpone imaginable.

are as enjoyable to look at as they are to eat, although portions do err on the small side. It's a more affordable alternative to legendary restaurant Cracco (p42). (☎ 02 837 39 63; www.carloecamillainsegheria. it; Via Giuseppe Meda; meals €48-56; ⊙ 6.30pm-2am; Ⓜ Romolo)

# Drinking

## Vinoir
WINE BAR

12 🚇 MAP P114, A4

This small, spare bar at the quieter end of the Navigli Grande harbours a generous and unusual selection of natural and biodynamic wines. Servers are knowledgeable and keen to share details of the wine's

provenance and character while bringing you delightful plates of Fassone *hosomaki* (sushi rolls) and octopus with smoked potato and black cabbage. (☎ 02 3981 1202; https://vinoir.com; Ripa di Porta Ticinese 93; ⊙ 10am-1pm & 5.30pm-midnight Tue-Sat, 7.30pm-midnight Mon; 🚋 160)

## VOLT
CLUB

13 🚇 MAP P114, D2

Owned by fashion guru Claudio Antonioli, this is possibly Milan's most beautiful club. Certainly, the fashion-forward punters look the part, set against a sleek all-black interior beneath lights tinted to match the mood of the night.

Thursday's Uptown party focuses on hip hop and R&B, while Friday's Mondrian night draws in big-name DJs and Saturday mellows out with electronica. (📞 table booking & guest list 342 7976858; www.voltclub.it; Via Molino delle Armi 16; €15-20; ⏰ 11.30pm-5am Thu-Sat; 🚊 3)

### Bar Rita                   COCKTAIL BAR

14 🚇 MAP P114, A4

This sleek American-style cocktail bar serves seriously creative cocktails and classics with a twist. Try the signature 'old-style' ne-groni with gin, Campari, Carpano and soda. Drinks come accompanied by delectable finger food like grilled octopus and aubergine, or burgers made with prime beef from the quality Masseroni butchery. (Via Fumagalli 1; cocktails €5-9; ⏰ 6.30pm-2am Mon-Sat; 🇲 Porta Genova)

### Mag Cafè                           BAR

15 🚇 MAP P114, B4

A Milanese speakeasy with wing-back armchairs, marble-topped tables, a patchwork of Persian rugs and huge lampshades that look like birds' nests. Like the decor, the drinks are creatively crafted, utilising interesting herbs and syrups, and served in vintage glassware – opt for the cocktail of the month, which is always a winner. Mag also does a popular brunch on weekends. (Ripa di Porta Ticinese 43; cocktails €7-9, brunch €10; ⏰ 7.30am-2am Mon-Fri, 9am-2am Sat & Sun; 🚊 2, 9)

### Ugo                        COCKTAIL BAR

16 🚇 MAP P114, B3

Hipster home Ugo has a retro vibe that will appeal to latter-day Gatsbys who find themselves in need of a rum or a bourbon-based cocktail such as the Little Easy (whisky, Peychard, orange bitters and absinthe). Accompany with the classic American burger made with superior Fassone beef (€14). (📞 02 3981 1557; www.ugobar.it; Via Corsico 12; cocktails €8; ⏰ 6pm-2am Tue-Sun; 🇲 Porta Genova)

### Rocket                            CLUB

17 🚇 MAP P114, A4

Courting an alternative, gay-friendly scene, Rocket is a local favourite that delivers a great DJ line-up, great cocktails and a load of unpretentious fun. It's famous for its three main nights: Void (electronic), Alphabet (transgressive) and extravagantly named Akeem of Zamunda (hip-hop, R&B and electronic). Once a month there's also a Sabotage night featuring international DJs. (📞 333 3313817; https://en-gb.facebook.com/rocketmilano; Alzaia Naviglio Grande 98; ⏰ 11.30pm-5am Thu-Sat; 🇲 Porta Genova)

# Entertainment

### Auditorium di Milano           CLASSICAL MUSIC

18 ⭐ MAP P114, C5

Abandoned after WWII, the Cinema Massimo was transformed

in 1999 into the state-of-the-art home of Milan's legendary Giuseppe Verde Symphonic Orchestra and Milan Chorus, as well as a venue for visiting international jazz acts and chamber music groups. (☎02 8338 9401; www.laverdi.org; Largo Gustav Mahler; ◷box office 10am-7pm Tue-Sun; 🚊3, 9)

### Nidaba Theatre
LIVE MUSIC

**19** ⭐ MAP P114, B4

This tiny, unpretentious venue down the heavily graffitied Via Gola has an outsized reputation for hosting stellar live-music performances for serious blues, soul, folk and rock-and-roll bands. Even better, admission is (amazingly) free – if you can squeeze in. (☎339 3477512; www.nidaba.it; Via Gola 12; admission free; ◷9pm-3am Tue-Sat; 🚊3, 9)

# Shopping

### Biffi
FASHION & ACCESSORIES

Retailer Rosy Biffi spotted potential in the young Giorgio Armani and Gianni Versace long before they became household names. More recently, Biffi got Milanese women hooked onto US cult-brand jeans. She has a knack for interpreting edgier trends and making them work for conformist Milan. Check out her selection of international fashion heavyweights for both men and women at her shop around the corner from Tokuyoshi (see 10 ✖ Map p114, B2). (☎02 8311 6052; www.biffi.com; Corso Genova 5 & 6; ◷3-7.30pm Mon, 10am-7.30pm Tue-Sat; 🚊2, 14)

### Frip
MUSIC

**20** 🔒 MAP P114, C2

A husband-and-wife, DJ-stylist duo highlight some of Milan's most avant-garde looks and sounds. Look for super-wearable ACNE workwear and puffball sleeve shirts by Marques'Almeida or fun Peter Non shearling slippers; then head straight for the cool selection of magazines and vinyl. (☎02 832 13 60; www.frip.it; Corso di Porta Ticinese 16; ◷3.30-8pm Mon, 11am-2pm & 3.30-8pm Tue-Sat; 🚊3)

### Foto Veneta Ottica
VINTAGE

**21** 🔒 MAP P114, D1

This 1930s studio is a blast from the past with its wood-framed cabinets packed with frames, ranging from vintage '60s butterfly lenses to chic modern labels like Germano Gambini. A leading European purveyor of vintage eyewear, the frames have even made the pages of *Vogue*. Find a superstar pair and have them snap a new passport picture. (☎02 805 57 35; www.fotovenetaottica.com; 1st fl, Via Torino 57; ◷9am-12.30pm & 3-7.20pm Mon-Sat; 🚊2, 14)

### Wok
FASHION & ACCESSORIES

**22** 🔒 MAP P114, D3

This is where the hip and affluent crowd of Milan go to maintain their on-trend wardrobes. It has an eclectic selection that mixes up avant-garde, emerging and street labels. You'll definitely spot items by A.P.C. and Maison

Margiela, along with a wall devoted to Retrosuperfuture sunnies. Wok also hosts art, design and fashion events. (☎02 8982 9700; www.wok-store.com; Viale Col di Lana 5a; ⊙3-7.45pm Mon, noon-7.45pm Tue-Fri, 10.30am-7.45pm Sat; ☷9)

## Stiù
SHOES

### 23 🅐 MAP P114, C3

Billed as a creative lab for emerging designers, Stiù stocks shoes that are often bold and always on trend. Along with the likes of Swedish Vagabond and LA brand Intentionally Blank, it has its own brand dedicated to original, cutting-edge designs. It caters mostly for women, but men will find a slimmer, well-curated selection. (☎02 551 76 20; www.stiushoes.com; Corso di Porta Ticinese 105; ⊙11am-2pm & 3-8pm Tue-Fri, 11am-8pm Sat, 2.30-8pm Sun; ☷62, 91, 92)

## Dictionary
CLOTHING

### 24 🅐 MAP P114, C2

Owned by a former skateboarder, this independent clothing store has a clean minimal style that walks the line between elegant and street. Its curated selection focuses on northern European brands such as Wood Wood and Sandqvist, along with other choice international and emerging brands. (☎02 835 82 12; www.dictionarymilano.it; Corso di Porta Ticinese 46; ⊙3.30-7.30pm Mon, 10.30am-7.30pm Tue-Fri, to 8pm Sat, 1.30-7.30pm Sun; ☷3)

Navigli Shopping

**Biffi (p120)**

# Walking Tour 🥾

# Zona Tortona

*Once a tangle of working-class tenements and factories, Zona Tortona is now flush with design companies, studios and neighbourhood eateries. This is home to the head offices of Diesel and Armani (look for the Tadao Ando–designed Armani Teatro on Via Bergognone). During April's Salone del Mobile (Furniture Fair), the area hosts satellite shows, launches and parties, transforming into a destination in itself.*

## Getting There

Ⓜ Take the M2 (green line) to Porta Genova, then take Via Ventimiglia to the left of the station and cross the tracks at the iron bridge.

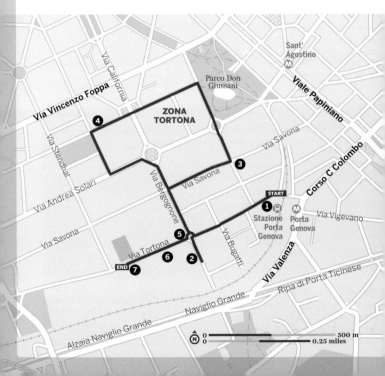

## ➊ Coffee at Cafè del Binari

Named after the railway tracks that drove modernity through Milan, Liberty-style **Cafè del Binari** (02 8940 6753; Via Tortona 3; 8am-6pm; Porta Genova) reflects the glamour of the railway age. Plump red tub chairs and a carved mahogany bar transport you to a more gracious age.

## ➋ Armani Silos

When Italian *Vogue* art director Flavio Lucchini opened a photographic studio on Via Tortona in 1983, everyone thought he was mad. But now 'the zone' is a magnet for designers, artists and photographers. No wonder Giorgio Armani opened his legacy museum, **Armani Silos** (02 9163 0010; www.armanisilos.com; Via Bergognone 40; adult/reduced €12/8.40; 11am-7pm Wed-Sun; Porta Genova), here.

## ➌ Fashionable Lunches

While the rest of Tortona modernises, **Trattoria Aurora** (02 832 3144; www.trattoriaauroramilano. it; Via Savona 23; meals €40-45; 12.30-2.30pm & 8-11pm; Porta Genova) firmly resists fashion fads. Starched tablecloths and excellent Piedmontese cuisine mollify even the most avant-garde fashionistas.

## ➍ Concept Shopping

Brainchild of Sardinian fashion designer Antonio Marras, **Non-ostanteMarras** (393 8934340; Via Cola di Rienzo 8; 10am-7pm Mon-Sat, noon-7pm Sun; 14) is an eccentric concept store hidden in an ivy-draped courtyard. It's full of magpie artefacts that sit alongside Marras' creative high-fashion clothing.

## ➎ Meet the Creatives

If you're wondering where all those hardworking creatives disappear to at the end of the day, drop into the bistro at co-working **Casa Base** (http://base.milano.it; Via Bergognone 34; dm with/without bathroom €55/35, d €90-120; Porta Genova).

## ➏ Design at Large

During Milan's annual Salone del Mobile furniture fair, Zona Tortona turns into an outdoor gallery and party venue thanks to the fringe fair, Fuorisalone (https://fuorisa lone.it/). Some of the best events are held at **Superstudio Più** (02 42 25 01; www.superstudiogroup.com; Via Tortona 27; hours vary; Porta Genova).

## ➐ Cocktails & Tapas

When you've exhausted the Salone's shows, retreat to the glasshouse harbouring the **Botanical Club** (02 423 28 90; www.thebotanicalclub.com; Via Tortona 33; cocktails €9-11, meals €25-45; 12.30-2.30pm & 6.30pm-2am Mon-Fri, 6.30pm-2am Sat, 12.30-3pm Sun; Porta Genova), a sleek restaurant, cocktail bar and microdistillery.

# Explore ⊕
# Porta Romana & Porta Vittoria

*Porta Romana and Porta Vittoria are popular residential areas, filled with art nouveau apartment blocks and good-value restaurants and bars. The triumphal Roman arch, built by Phillip III of Spain in 1596, remains at Porta Romana, but neither neighbourhood has a centre or scene, although the gleaming addition of Fondazione Prada is is increasing the area's popularity.*

*Start the day exploring Porta Vittoria, hunting down excellent pastries at Sissi (p128). In between, you can browse small boutiques and vintage stores. Then wander south down tree-lined residential streets. Along the way, you can visit the fresco-filled Santa Maria dei Miracoli e San Celso (p127) and the hectagonal garden of Rotonda della Besana (p127), where you can stop for a spritz or a picnic.Then, head to the far south of Porta Romana for cutting-edge contemporary art at the Fondazione Prada (p127). This will put you in the right place for some excellent aperitivi and dinner options after which you can dance the night away at Santeria Social Club (p132).*

## Getting There & Around

Ⓜ For the QC Terme spa (www.termemilano.com) and I Bagni Misteriosi pools, exit at Porta Romana on M3 (yellow line); for Fondazione Prada continue to Lodi TIBB on the M3.

🚋 No. 9 travels around Viale Premuda giving access to the Rotonda della Besana; while trams 12 and 27 travel along Corso di Porta Vittoria and Corso XXII Marzo.

**Porta Romana & Porta Vittoria Map on 126**

Chiesa di San Bernardino alle Ossa (p128) POSZTOS/SHUTTERSTOCK ©

A

B

C

D

1

Via A Marzoni

Montenapoleone

Via Senato

M Palestro

Viale Piave

Via Carlo Goldoni

Via Fratelli Bronzetti

Piazza Risorgimento

Via Pietro Verri

Corso Venezia

17

6

Via Macedonio Melloni

San Babila M

Corso Monforte

Via Pietro Mascagni

Via Benvenuto Cellini

14

Via Pasquale Sottocorno

21 Dateo

Via U Visconti di Modrone

Via Filippo Corridoni

Via Archimede

2

5

20

Via Fiamma

Via Marcona

Piazza Emilia

Chiesa di San Bernardino alle Ossa

Corso di Porta Vittoria

Piazza Cinque Giornate

Corso XXII Marzo

4

Missori M

Via Francesco Sforza

Giardino della Guastalla

Rotonda della Besana

Via Fontana

Via Spartaco

Largo Marinai d'Italia

Torre Velasca

3

Via della Commenda

Viale Regina Margherita

PORTA ROMANA

10

Via Cadore

3

Via Santa Sofia

Crocetta

Via A Lamarmora

Via Pace

Viale Emilio Caldara

Via Andrea Maffei

Via Fogazzaro

Via Bergamo

Via Simone D'Orsenigo

22

Corso Italia

Via G Mercalli

23

Via Orti

Piazzale Libia

Via Comelico

16

2

Chiesa di Santa Maria dei Miracoli e San Celso

Corso di Porta Romana

Via S Martino

18

Via Pier Lombardo

Via Tirabaschi

Via Sigieri

Cirene

Viale Umbria

Via Tito Livio

Corso Italia/Via Lusardi

Viale Beatrice d'Este

9

Via S Lattuada

11

4

Viale Bligny

13

Porta Romana

12

Via Lodovico Muratori

Viale Pietro Colletta

Via Salasco

8

PORTA ROMANA

Via Crema

15

Via L Papi

Via F Bocconi

Via G Bellezza

Via G Romano

Via Piacenza

7

Corso Lodi

Via R Sarfatti

Parco Ravizza

Via Palladio

Viale Isonzo

Porta Romana

Via Leo Longanesi

Viale Toscana

19

Lodi TIBB M

Corso Lodi

5

Via Carlo Bazzi

Via Spadolini

Via G Lorenzini

Largo Isarco Fondazione Prada

Via Brembo

1

Via Bernardino Verro

Via G Ripamonti

Via dei Fontanili

Via Oglio

Viale Ortles

For reviews see

| | | |
|---|---|---|
| ◉ Sights | p127 |
| ✕ Eating | p128 |
| ☕ Drinking | p131 |
| Entertainment | p132 |
| Shopping | p133 |

6

Via Barletta

N

0          500 m
0        0.25 miles

A

B

C

D

# Sights

### Fondazione Prada    GALLERY

**1** ⊙ MAP P126, C5

Conceived by designer Miuccia Prada and architect Rem Koolhaas, this museum is as innovative and creative as the minds that gave it shape. Seven renovated buildings and three new structures have transformed a dilapidated former brandy factory into 19,000 sq m of exciting, multilevel exhibition space. The buildings, including a four-storey Haunted House tower clad in gold leaf, work seamlessly together, presenting some stunning visual perspectives. (www.fondazioneprada.org; Largo Isarco 2; adult/reduced €10/8; ⊙10am-7pm Mon, Wed & Thu, to 8pm Fri-Sun; MLodi TIBB)

### Chiesa di Santa Maria dei Miracoli e San Celso    CHURCH

**2** ⊙ MAP P126, A3

This church's Renaissance facade festooned with statues seems distinctly un-Milanese with its gleaming Carrara marble and mannerist extravagance, but after the Duomo and Sant'Ambrogio it holds a special place in Milanese hearts thanks to its miracle-performing, 15th-century fresco of the *Madonna and Child* in the left aisle. Inside, lavish Renaissance frescoes by Bergognone, Procaccini and Appiani give the interior a technicolour glow and newlyweds still flock here to leave a token bouquet of flowers for a happy life

together. (www.santamariadeimiracoliesancelso.it; Corso Italia 37; admission free; ⊙10am-noon & 4-5.30pm Mon-Wed, Fri & Sat, 4-6pm Sun; MMissori)

### Rotonda della Besana    GARDENS

**3** ⊙ MAP P126, C3

It's said this former cemetery to the poor was once the burial site for nearly 150,000 people. Now it's the charming setting for a picnic, read or wander, and houses the children's museum **MUBA** (www.muba.it; Via Enrico Besana 12; adult/child/family of 4 €6/8/25; ⊙9.30am-5pm Tue-Sun; 👶; 🚋9) along with a chic cafe. It's round (as the name suggests), in late baroque style with a repurposed chapel at the centre and charming porticos lining its walls. (Via Enrico Besana 12; admission free; 🚋9)

---

### Torre Velasca

Studio BBPR's 1958 skyscraper, the **Torre Velasca** (Map p126, A3; Piazza Velasca; MMissori), is an iconic Milanese landmark. The top-heavy tower camply tilts at Castello Sforzesco and the Duomo's lovely buttresses. Slightly sinister, ever so sci-fi and cleverly maximising use of available footprint, it's Lombard to the core. Sadly, apart from the foyer, it's currently as unbreachable as the medieval fortresses it emulates.

## Chiesa di San Bernardino alle Ossa

CHURCH, OSSUARY

4  MAP P126, B2

This church dates from the 13th century, when its ossuary was used to bury plague victims from nearby San Barnaba hospital. It was rebuilt in rococo style in 1679, after it collapsed beneath the fallen bell tower of adjacent Santo Stefano. The walls of the new ossuary, with its frescoed vault, *Triumph of Souls among Flying Angels,* are now lined with a macabre flourish in human bones, finished with the skulls of condemned prisoners. (Via Carlo Giuseppe Merlo 4; admission free; 8am-noon & 1-6pm Mon-Fri, 9.30am-6pm Sat; Duomo)

# Eating

## Pavè Ice-cream

GELATO $

5 MAP P126, B2

As the sibling of *pasticceria* (pastry shop) phenomenon, Pavè (p57), you can expect great things from this contemporary gelateria with its marble-topped counters and stainless steel tubs of ice cream that look like an artist's paint palette. Gelato-genius Simona Carmagnola's boundary-pushing flavours include coffee and cardamom, spicy tonka bean and a taste-tingling rocket-and-lime sorbet. It also offers some quality vegan options. (02 876 4530; www.pavemilano.com; Via Cesare Battisti 21; scoops €2.50-4; noon-10pm; ; 12, 19, 27)

## Pasticceria Sissi

PASTRIES $

6 MAP P126, C1

There's nothing more Milanese than breakfast at Sissi. Yet, with its bright pink walls, vintage posters and an Italian-Senegalese owner with a big personality, this isn't just your classic *pasticceria.* You'll have to push past the fur coats of the *sciure* (posh Milanese women) to order its famous sweets and croissants, but they're worth it. (02 7601 4664; Piazza Risorgimento 6; pastries €1.30-4, cake €6-7; 6.30am-noon Mon, to 8pm Wed-Sun; 9)

## Giannasi dal 1967

FAST FOOD $

7 MAP P126, C4

Since 1967, Dorando Giannasi has been serving Milan's best roast chicken from his food stall on Piazza Buozzi. Marinated in a secret herb mix and broiled in the kitchen across the street, the savoury smells draw throngs at lunchtime. Vegetable skewers, potatoes with rosemary, arancini rice balls and English-style roast beef are all available to take away or eat at the counter. (02 5832 1114; http://giannasi1967.it; Piazza Bruno Buozzi; half-chicken €2.50; 7am-8pm Mon-Sat; Porta Romana)

## Trattoria del Pescatore

SEAFOOD $$

8 MAP P126, B4

Milan's finest fish restaurant hides modestly behind a row of green awnings. At the helm are Sardinian couple Giuliano and Agnese and their son, who interned at three-Michelin-starred Arzak in San Sebastián. The pasta is handmade in their home town and the unmissable signature dish is the Catalan lobster drowned in Camone tomatoes and Tropea onions. Finish with green-apple sorbet and Sardinian cheeses. (☎02 5832 0452; www.trattoriadelpescatore.it; Via Atto Vannucci 5; meals €40-45; ⏱12.30-2.30pm & 8-11pm Mon-Sat; Ⓜ Porta Romana)

### Trattoria Trippa ITALIAN $$

9 ❌ MAP P126, C4

Having honed his skills at Michelin-starred St Hubertus in the Dolomites, chef Diego Rossi and blogger Peter Caroli now have their own restaurant. As the name suggests, tripe features heavily on the menu alongside historic recipes using eel, wild greens, char, rabbit and even snails. The quality of the ingredients is superlative and there's an interesting organic wine list. (☎327 668/908; www.trippamilano.it; Via Giorgio Vasari 3; meals €30-40; ⏱7.30-11.30pm Mon-Sat; Ⓜ Porta Romana)

### Pasticceria KNAM PASTRIES $$

10 ❌ MAP P126, D3

Opened by celebrated German chef Ernst Knam, this is one of the most famous pastry shops in the city. Known for its unusual flavour pairings and chocolate desserts (Knam isn't called 'the King of Chocolate' for nothing), it also has its own version of the locally loved Christmas *panettone* (a yeast-risen sweet bread), renamed Knamettone. (☎02 5519 4448; www.eknam.com; Via Augusto Anfossi 10; small

Fondazione Prada, designed by architect Rem Koolhaas (p127)

Porta Romana & Porta Vittoria Eating

cakes & pastries from €6, individual chocolate €1.50; ⏲10am-1pm Tue-Sun, 4-8pm Mon-Fri, 3-8pm Sat; 🚌73)

## Un Posto a Milano

MODERN ITALIAN $$

11 ❌ MAP P126, D4

This country *cascina* (farmstead) was a derelict ruin until a collection of cooperatives and cultural associations returned it to multifunctional use as restaurant, bar, social hub and **guesthouse** (📞02 545 7785; www. unpostoamilano.it; Via Cuccagna 2; s €70-115, d €90-144, qd €284; 🛜; Ⓜ Porta Romana). Delicious salads, homemade focaccia, soups and snacks are served throughout the day at the bar, while the restaurant serves simple home cooking using locally sourced ingredients. (📞02 545 77 85; www. unpostoamilano.it; Via Cuccagna 2; meals

€15-35; ⏲12.30-2.30pm & 7.30-11pm Tue-Sun; 🍷🚻; Ⓜ Porta Romana)

## Pastamadre

SICILIAN $$

12 ❌ MAP P126, C4

Named after the natural yeast base used by master pastry chefs for more than a century, this Sicilian bakery and restaurant makes a powerful statement about simple, good food. Order organic breads, croissants and puff-pastries stuffed with strawberry *frangipane* (pastry) from a bar made of wooden boxes beneath a ceiling of cardboard tubes. Lunch means housemade pasta dressed in Sicilian sauces such as stewed octopus. (📞02 5519 0020; Via Bernardino Corio 8; meals €25-35; ⏲noon-3pm & 7-11pm Mon-Sat, noon-3pm Sun; Ⓜ Porta Romana)

Pasticceria KNAM (p129)

## Potaflori ITALIAN $$

13 MAP P126, B4

Beautiful Potaflori run by jazz
singer and florist Rosalba Piccinni
is full of flowers, food and fun. In
the morning, long stone benches
are laden with pastries beneath
glass domes before the lunchtime
crowd arrives for plates of quinoa
salad on lacquered tables. The
mood changes again come *aperitivo* time when glasses of *spritz*
are accompanied by outbursts of
piano playing and song. (02 8706
5930; www.potafiori.com; Via Salasco
17; meals €30-45; 9am-midnight
Mon-Sat, 5pm-midnight Sun; 9)

## Ristorante
da Giacomo SEAFOOD $$$

14 MAP P126, C2

This sunny Tuscan restaurant
serves up an elegant, unpreten-
tious menu featuring largely fish
and shellfish. Start with a slice of
sardine-and-caper pizza and follow
with the fresh linguine with scampi
and the oven-baked sea bass.
(02 7602 3313; www.giacomoris
torante.com; Via Pasquale Sottocorno
6; meals €50-60; 12.30-2.30pm &
7.30-11.30pm; 9, 23)

# Drinking

## Spirit COCKTAIL BAR

15 MAP P126, C4

From the metal-studded door with
its mysterious porthole to the sleek,
sweeping wooden bar and canary-
yellow bar stools, the Spirit is a

serious and supersexy cocktail bar.
Every fortnight, bar manager Luca
Bacchi and his team conjure up a
list of unique signature cocktails,
which they serve alongside exclu-
sive rums like Ron Gran, Japanese
whiskies and rare Pechuga mezcal.
(02 8457 0612; www.thespirit.it;
Via Piacenza 15; 6pm-2am Tue-Sun;
Porta Romana)

## LambicZoon BAR

16 MAP P126, D3

This craft-beer bar has won a slew
of awards for its unusual celebra-
tion of wild fermented beers,
imported Belgian brands and
interesting Italian sour ales like
the citrusy Flos Alba Bergamotto
from Birrificio Italiano. Downstairs
there's a restaurant serving burg-
ers and meat-and-cheese platters,
and there's a small outdoor patio.
(02 3653 4840; www.lambiczoon.
com; Via Friuli 46; 6.30pm-2am
Mon-Fri, 12.30-3pm Sat, 6.30pm-1am
Sun; 16)

## Nottingham Forest COCKTAIL BAR

17 MAP P126, C1

If Michelin awarded stars for bars,
Nottingham Forest would have
one. This eclectically decorated
Asian/African tiki bar named after
an English football team is the out-
post of molecular mixologist Dario
Comino, who conjures smoking
cocktails packed with dry ice and
ingenuity. Unique cocktails include
the Elite, a mix of vodka, ground
pearls and sake – supposedly an
aphrodisiac. (www.nottingham-forest.

### Lido
### Lifestyle

Conceived as a community hub by architect Luigi Secchi in 1939, **I Bagni Misteriosi** (📞02 8973 1800; www.bagnimisteriosi.com; Via Carlo Botta 18; adult/reduced €7-15/5-12 depending on time of day; 🕙10am-6pm Sun-Mon & Wed, 10am-midnight Thu, 10am-10pm Fri & Sat; 🚻; Ⓜ Porta Romana) is a beautiful modernist *lido* with vast heated pools, close-cropped lawns, shaded porticos, a bistro and bar. Painstakingly restored, and reopened in 2017, it is once again a favourite summer social hub. Besides the swimming, there's tai chi, art classes, evening *aperitivo*, and dance and music concerts hosted by the adjoining Teatro Franco Parenti (p132) on a floating stage.

The best time to visit is between 6.30pm and 9pm for an unforgettable *aperitivo* around the pools.

com; Viale Piave 1; cocktails €10; 🕙6.30pm-2am Tue-Sat, 6pm-1am Sun; 🚌9, 23)

# Entertainment

## Teatro Franco Parenti THEATRE

18 ⭐ MAP P126, C3

Having made a name for itself with a program boasting some of the finest names in Italian cinema and theatre, Franco Parenti cemented its role as a community hub with the opening of I Bagni Misteriosi (p132). Aside from theatre, there are concerts, film screenings, book readings and a variety of outdoor events. (📞02 5999 5206; www.teatrofrancoparenti.it; Via Pier Lombardo 14; Ⓜ Porta Romana)

## Santeria Social Club CLUB

19 ⭐ MAP P126, A5

Multifunctional spaces are all the rage in Milan, and Santeria encap-sulates the mood perfectly. By day this ex-Volvo dealership acts as a co-working space, classroom (with courses in music communications, marketing and bartending) and restaurant, before turning into one of the city's hottest bars hosting live music and cultural events at night. (📞02 2219 9381; www.santeria.milano.it/toscana; Viale Toscana 18; 🕙11am-1am Sun & Mon, to 2am Tue-Thu, to 3am Fri & Sat; 🚌90)

## Conservatorio di Musica Giuseppe Verdi CLASSICAL MUSIC

20 ⭐ MAP P126, C2

Housed in a former Lateran convent, Milan's most prestigious musical conservatory and high school has nurtured some of the country's best conductors and musicians. Although named after the great composer Giuseppe Verdi, he himself was rejected from the school. Now chamber music events and symphonic concerts are held in two halls, the Sala Puccini and Sala Verdi. (📞02 76 21 10; www.consmilano.it; Via Conservatorio 12; MSan Babila)

# Shopping

## Altalen
HATS

Milan's hottest new milliners are Antonina Nafi de Luca and Elena Todros, who artfully craft Madagascan straw golf hats, towering silk turbans and custom-made berets at their tiny atelier, near Ristorante da Giacomo (see 14 ✕ Map p126, C2). Their unique creations, many inspired by scenes from cinema or theatre, have won them regular outings on the fashion show circuit, although their felt fedoras and foldable straw sun hats are perfect for everyday wear. (📞02 8703 4435; www.altalen.it; Via Benvenuto Cellini 21; ⏰10.30am-1.30pm & 3.30-7.30pm Tue-Fri, Sat by appt; 🚋9)

## Mania Vintage
VINTAGE

21 🅰 MAP P126, D2

Serious handbag aficionados need look no further than this superbly curated vintage store, which specialises in bags and accessories from high-end brands such as Chanel, Louis Vuitton, Hermès and Prada with limited editions stored in glass cabinets. Owner Roberto is a passionate collector and insists on authenticating each item. For those interested in rare

Kelly bags, payment in instalments is possible. (📞02 8708 8040; www.maniavintage.it; Via Fratelli Bronzetti 11; ⏰3.30-7.30pm Mon, 10am-7.30pm Tue-Sat; 🚋12, 27)

## Camiceria Olga
CLOTHING

22 🅰 MAP P126, D3

Although Milan made prêt-à-porter fashionable in the 1960s, the made-to-measure habit remained ingrained and most Milanese have a personal seamstress or tailor to conjure their perfectly fitted clothes. Get in on the act, at this affordable shirtmaker which turns out custom-tailored shirts in plains and pinstripes or even raw silk and cashmere. Appointments aren't required and it ships globally. (📞02 4547 8092; www.camiceriaolga.it; Via Comelico 3; ⏰8.30am-6pm Mon-Fri, 8.30am-12.30pm Sat; 🚋16)

## Ciasmo
FASHION & ACCESSORIES

23 🅰 MAP P126, B3

With two nimble-fingered seamstresses for grandmothers, it's unsurprising that Sara Scaramuzza's fashion and homewares showroom is full of colourful, creative pieces. Suits and dresses can be made to measure, or you may come away with a Japanese fabric umbrella, a pimped-up straw hat or a delightful paper sculpture. (📞339 8693593; https://ciasmodotit.wordpress.com; Via Orti 7; ⏰10am-1.30pm & 3-7.30pm Tue-Sat; MCrocetta)

## Worth a Trip 👀
# Borromean Islands

*Forming Lake Maggiore's most beautiful corner, the Borromean Islands (Isole Borromee) are still owned by the aristocratic Borromeo family. They have owned these islands (they own six of the lake's nine islands) since the 17th century and still summer here in the stunning Palazzo Borromeo. Three of the four islands – Bella, Madre and Superiore (aka Isola dei Pescatori) – can all be visited, but tiny San Giovanni is off limits.*

📞 0323 3 05 56

www.isoleborromee.it

adult/child €16/8.50, incl Palazzo Madre €21/10

🕑 9am-5.30pm mid-Mar–mid-Oct

# Isola Bella

Isola Bella (pictured left) is the centrepiece of the Borromean archipelago. The island took the name of Carlo III's wife, the *bella* Isabella, when Count Carlo Borromeo III commissioned a vast palace situated in an exotic garden for the Borromeo family. Built on a barren island between 1632 and 1671, it is Count Borromeo's version of the Garden of Hesperides, that blissful orchard of classical mythology where immortality-giving golden apples grew.

For those who want to experience the magic of the island after dark, **Elvezia** (📞0323 3 00 43; Via de Martini 35; meals €32-42; ⏰9am-6pm Tue-Sun Mar-Oct, Fri-Sun only Nov-Feb) has seven elegant bedrooms (d €134 to €170). It's also the best place to eat on the island, with outdoor dining beneath a flower-laden pergola. Dishes include ricotta-stuffed ravioli, risotto and lake fish such as *coregone alle mandorle* (lake white-fish in almonds).

## Palazzo Borromeo

Palazzo Borromeo is the finest building on Lake Maggiore and sits atop an extraordinary tiered garden. Count Carlo's vision was for a pyramid of terraces that would mimic the shape of a galleon at anchor. The island's handful of inhabitants, who were asked to relocate from their homes, understandably didn't share the Count's enthusiasms so plans had to be modified and the galleon lost its pointed prow. Nevertheless, it still has the appearance of a ship afloat in the lake.

Inside, its ornate halls and guest rooms are lavishly decorated and filled with the finest artworks. Particularly striking rooms include the Sala di Napoleone, where the emperor Napoleon stayed with his wife in 1797; the grand Sala da Ballo (Ballroom); the ornate Sala del Trono (Throne Room); and the Sala delle Regine (Queens' Room).

## ★ Top Tips

To beat the crowds, get an early morning start when visiting the Borromean Islands. If you plan to visit all three islands from either Verbania or Stresa, buy a day ticket for €17 – it's a round-trip ticket that includes stops in Verbania, Stresa, Baveno and the three Borromean islands.

## ✕ Take a Break

Isola Bella has a few eating choices – including a cafe on the grounds of Palazzo Borromeo. The best option is Elvezia.

Otherwise, visitors make a quick hop to Isola Superiore. Casabella (p137) is situated right by the shoreline.

## ★ Getting There

From Milan there are hourly trains to Stresa (from €8.50, 1¼ hours).

Ferries run every half-hour or so from Stresa to Isola Bella (€7 return, five to 10 minutes).

Within the palace, a museum within a museum showcases the 130-strong Borromeo collection of Old Masters. Highlights include Rubens, Titian, Paolo Veronese, Andrea Mantegna, Van Dyck and José Ribera (Spagnoletto). You'll also find Flemish tapestries, sculptures by Antonio Canova and – in the Salone Grande – a 200-year-old wooden model of the palace and island.

## The Garden

Outside the extravagance continues, in what is Italy's finest baroque garden designed by Angelo Crivelli. Fountains, grottoes and a water theatre combine to form a theatrical and energetic space. Vast quantities of soil were ferried from the mainland to clothe the jagged rock with 10 sloping terraces. Marble from Baveno followed and stone

from Viggiù. Later, boats packed with Spanish lemon trees, lilies and lotus flowers brought the flora for its rising galleries and, finally, statues of Agriculture and Arts, waving putti and the triumphant Borromeo unicorns were set atop Carlo Fontana's shell-encrusted water theatre. It is the perfect expression of the confidence and power of the Borromean family who furnished Milan with two cardinals, one of whom was canonised by Pope Paul V in 1610.

## Isola Madre

The largest island in the Borromean archipelago, Isola Madre's entire 7.8 hectares is devoted to a delightful botanic garden, one of the oldest in Italy. The island's benign microclimate favours the growth of wisteria, rare subtropical plants and

Isola Superiore

## Garden Pioneers

Plantsmen rather than architects were the heroes of 19th-century gardens thanks to gardeners such as the Rovelli brothers, who worked for the Borromean family. Experts in cultivation and hybridisation, the brothers ran a nursery on the sidelines at Verbania Pallanza, where they sold some of the Count's 500 varieties of camellia alongside gardening catalogues. This growing exchange of information popularised gardening as a pastime and throughout the 19th century nurseries and horticultural societies proliferated around the lakes. This passion persists today as evidenced by the enthusiastic crowds at Lake Maggiore's **camellia festival** (☺Mar) and **Settimana del Tulipano** (☺Apr), a week dedicated to tulips, at **Villa Taranto** (📞0323 55 66 67; www.villataranto.it; Via Vittorio Veneto 111, Verbania Pallanza; adult/reduced €10/5.50; ☺8.30am-6.30pm Apr-Sep, 9am-4pm Oct; P).

exotic flowers and trees, the oldest being an enormous Kashmir cypress, which is over 200 years old.

### Palazzo Madre

Isola Madre is entirely taken up by the Palazzo Madre and the lovely gardens that surround it. The 16th- to 18th-century palace is a wonderfully decadent structure crammed full of all manner of antique furnishings and adornments. Highlights include Countess Borromeo's doll collection, a neoclassical puppet theatre designed by a scenographer from Milan's La Scala, and a 'horror' theatre with a cast of devilish marionettes.

## Isola Superiore

Tiny 'Fishermen's Island', with a permanent population of around 50, retains its fishing-village atmosphere. Apart from an 11th-century apse and a 16th-century fresco in the charming Chiesa di San Vittore, there are no sights. Instead, visitors make it their port of call for lunch. Restaurants cluster around the boat landing, all serving fish fresh from the lake.

Set at the southern tip of the island is **Albergo Verbano** (📞0323 3 04 08; www.hotelverbano.it; Via Ugo Ara 2; d €140-210; ☺Mar-Dec; 🛜). It has been putting guests up since 1895 and has a lovely waterside restaurant that serves a fish-focused menu. Another excellent waterside spot is **Casabella** (📞0323 3 34 71; www.isola-pescatori.it; Via del Marinaio 1; meals €30-50, 5-course tasting menu €55; ☺noon-2pm & 6-8.30pm Feb-Nov) where the menu includes home-smoked beef with spinach, blanched squid with ricotta and perfectly cooked lake fish. If you don't want to leave after dinner, there are two snug bedrooms (doubles from €110).

## Worth a Trip 🔭
# Como

*Sitting at the southern tip of its namesake lake, Como is a self-confident and historic town, established by Julius Caesar in the 1st century BC. Philosophers Pliny the Elder and Pliny the Younger were born here, and Virgil thought Como, with its narrow profile and soaring Alpine amphitheatre, the greatest Italian lake. Nowadays, Como is reimagining itself as the lake's coolest hub, full of hip hotels and good restaurants.*

### Getting There

🚆 Trains from Milan's Stazione Centrale to Como San Giovanni (€4.80 to €13.50, 37 to 90 minutes).

🚆 Trains from Milan's Cadorna FN to Como Nord Lago (€4.80, one hour, hourly).

# Duomo

Como's awesome marble-clad **cathedral** (Cattedrale di Como; ☑ 031 331 22 75; Piazza del Duomo; admission free; ☺9.30am-5.30pm Mon-Fri, 10.45am-4.30pm Sat, 1-4.30pm Sun) is one of the most important buildings on the lake, incorporating a variety of styles – Romanesque, Renaissance and Gothic topped by a rococo cupola – over its centuries-long construction between 1396 and 1770. Inside, Renaissance chapels flank the cross-vaulted nave, which is hung with huge tapestries that were woven in gold thread in Ferrara, Florence and Antwerp. Statues of Pliny the Elder and Pliny the Younger adorn the facade, an unusual honour for two humanist philosophers.

# Passeggiata Lino Gelpi

One of Como's most charming walks is the lakeside stroll west from Piazza Cavour. Passeggiata Lino Gelpi leads past the **Monumento ai Caduti** (Memorial; Viale Puecher 9; ☺3-6pm Sun summer), a 1931 memorial to Italy's WWI dead. Next you'll pass a series of mansions and villas, including **Villa Saporiti** (Via Borgo Vico 148) and **Villa Gallia** (Via Borgo Vico 154), both now owned by the provincial government and closed to the public, before arriving at the garden-ringed **Villa Olmo** (☑ 031 25 23 52; www.villaolmocomo.it; Via Cantoni 1; gardens free, villa entry varies by exhibition; ☺villa during exhibitions 10am-6pm Tue-Sun, gardens 8am-11pm Apr-Sep, to 7pm Oct-Mar).

# Basilica di San Fedele

Enclosing one side of what was once a medieval grain market, this Lombard Romanesque **basilica** (Piazza San Fedele; ☺8am-noon & 3.30-7pm) dates back to the 7th century, although what you see now was built in 1120 after the relics of Roman martyr San Fedele were entombed here in the altar. Inside, its three naves

★ **Top Tips**

○ Como's **tourist office** (☑ 031 30 41 37; www.visitcomo.eu; Via Albertolli 7; ☺10am-6pm) is stacked with information.

○ Buy a museum card (€10), which allows admission to Como's four civic museums.

✕ **Take a Break**

**Osteria del Gallo** (☑ 031 27 25 91; www.osteriadelgallo-como.it; Via Vitani 16; meals €26-32; ☺12.30-3pm Mon, to 10pm Tue-Sat) is a traditional trattoria with a menu of local dishes.

**Pronobis** (☑ 031 26 17 86; Via Lambertenghi 19; meals €15-30; ☺11am-3pm & 5.30-9pm Mon-Sat) wine bar offers a short menu and excellent wine pairings.

**Enoteca Castiglioni** (☑ 031 26 18 60; www.castiglionistore.com; Via Rovelli 17; ☺10am-8pm Mon, to 9pm Tue-Sat) is a heritage deli and wine merchant where you can sample first-rate vintages.

and apses are covered in 16th- and 17th-century frescoes; a handful of older ones also survive, including the *Beheading of San Fedele*.

## The Funicular

Prepare for some spectacular views. The **Como–Brunate funicular** ( [📞]031 30 36 08; www.funicolarecomo. it; Piazza de Gasperi 4; adult one-way/ return €3/5.50, reduced €2/3.20; [🕐]half-hourly departures 6am-midnight summer, to 10.30pm winter) and built in 1894 and takes seven minutes to trundle up to the quiet hilltop village of Brunate (720m), revealing a memorable panorama of mountains and lakes. From there a steep 30-minute walk along a stony track leads to San Maurizio (907m), where 143 steps climb to the top of a lighthouse.

### Christmas Fair

A great time to visit Como is during the Christmas Fair, **Citta del Balocchi** ( [🕐]25 Nov-7 Jan), which consists of dozens of activities, beautiful Christmas lights, and an ice rink and Christmas market in Piazza Cavour. Concerts take place around town, there's a fireworks display on New Year's Eve and the festival ends with the dramatic arrival of La Befana (Italy's present-bearing folkloric witch) swooping down into Piazza Duomo on Epiphany (6 January).

## Lido di Villa Olmo

What a delight: a compact **beach** ( [📞]031 338 48 54; www.lidovillaolmo. it; Via per Cernobbio 2; adult/reduced €9/5; [🕐]9am-7pm mid-May–Sep) where you can plunge into open-air pools, sunbathe beside the lake, rent boats, sip cocktails at the waterfront bar and soak up mountain views. Bliss. You'll have to bring a swim cap or purchase one here if you want to use the pool.

## Aero Club

For a true touch of glamour, take a tour in a seaplane with **Aero Club Como** ( [📞]031 57 44 95; www.aeroclub como.com; Viale Masia 44; 30-min flight per person €90) and buzz about the skies high above Como. The often bumpy take-off and landing on the lake itself is thrilling, as are the views down onto the villas and villages dotted far below. Flights are popular; book three or four days ahead in summer. Maximum group size four.

## Silk Museum

Lake Como's aspiring silk makers still learn their trade in the 1970s-built Istituto Tecnico Industriale di Setificio textile technical school. It's also home to the **Museo della Seta** (Silk Museum; [📞]031 30 31 80; www. museosetacomo.com; Via Castelnuovo 9; adult/reduced €10/7; [🕐]10am-6pm Tue-Fri, to 1pm Sat), which draws together the threads of the town's silk history. Early dyeing and printing equipment features amid displays that chart the production process.

N 0                   1 km
0                   0.5 miles

Lake Como

Via Torno

Lido di Villa Olmo

Villa Olmo

Piazza de Gasperi

Funicolare Como-Brunate

Villa Gallia

Passeggiata Lino Gelpi

Monumento ai Caduti

Piazza Matteotti

Como Lago

Villa Saporiti

Aero Club Como

Sinigaglia Stadium

Piazza Cavour

Tourist Office

Piazza Grimoldi

Duomo

Teatro Sociale

Via Borgo Vico

Osteria del Gallo

Lopez Vintage

Piazzale San Gottardo

Como San Giovanni

Piazza Mazzini

Pronobis

Piazza San Fedele

Basilica di San Fedele

18 del Pero

Enoteca Castiglioni

Viale Innocenzo XI

Pinacoteca Civica

Piazza Vittoria

Mercato Coperto

Como Borghi

Via C Battisti

Piazzale Gerbetto

Via Cigalini

Basilica di Sant'Abbondio

Via Morazzone

Via Castelnuovo

Musco della Seta

Via Regina Theodolinda

Via Milano

## Silk Souvenirs

**18 del Pero** (📞031 24 23 55; www.18delpero.com; Via Adamo del Pero 18; ⏰9.30am-1.30pm & 3-7.30pm Tue-Sat) is a smart little shop run by designer Simona Trombetta, who is responsible for much of the well-priced contemporary jewellery made with brass, bronze, silver and freshwater pearls that is on sale here. Other tempting items are the handmade straw hats, and a small, beautifully curated selection of Como silk scarves.

## Basilica di Sant'Abbondio

About 500m south of Como's city walls is this austere 11th-century Romanesque **basilica** (Via Regina; ⏰8am-6pm summer, to 4.30pm winter), once the seat of a bishopric built on the orders of St Amantius of Como in order to house precious relics of no less than Sts Peter and Saint Paul. The highlights are the soaring frescoes inside the apse that depict scenes from the life of Christ, from the Annunciation to his burial. The adjoining cloister is now home to a law faculty.

## Teatro Sociale

Como's neoclassical **theatre** (📞031 27 01 70; www.teatrosocialecomo.it; Piazza Verdi) attracts culture vultures from as far away as Switzerland and has been enlarged three times to its present 900-seat capacity to accommodate them. Throughout the winter it hosts a fantastic program of opera, dance and even pop concerts. Free musical recitals are

Villa Olmo gardens (p139)

## Como's Silk History

Smuggled out of China inside a bamboo pole, the first silkworms reached northern Italy in the 13th century. At the time, the majority of peasants around Lake Como were employed in woollen mills, but given the abundance of mulberry trees in the Po valley a few canny entrepreneurs, such as Pietro Boldoni, spotted the potential for sericulture and established Como's first silk spinning mill in the early 1500s.

Although nurturing the worms and harvesting the silk was brutally hard work, silk cultivation gradually became an annual sideline for lower- and middle-class families, many of whom risked their annual savings trying to capitalise on the rich harvest. Entire sections of farmhouses were turned over to the worms, which women and children tirelessly fed mulberry leaves by hand until they spun their silken cocoons. To make just one tie, a hundred cocoons were needed.

held monthly on a Sunday in the beautiful Sala Bianca at 11am.

## Covered Market

Como's largest and best food market is this Fascist-era **covered market** (Via Mentana 5; ⏰8am-1pm Tue & Thu, to 7pm Fri & Sat) crammed with fruit, veg, meat, bread and cheese purveyors. One hall is entirely devoted to organic, local produce that has to come from a defined area around the city. Here you'll find lake fish, mountain honey and rare, small-batch Lombard cheeses.

## Vintage Shopping

On one of Como's most atmospheric streets, **Lopez Vintage** (📞031 24 20 43; Via Vitani 32; ⏰10am-12.30pm & 3.30-7pm Tue-Sat) lures you in with its whimsical window displays. Inside, the tiny jewel box of a shop has elegant vintage pieces – slim-fitting dresses, over-sized sunglasses, hats, accessories and other eye candy. Prices can be high, but you'll discover unique outfits, hats and jewellery you won't find elsewhere.

## Civic Art Gallery

Despite its inadequate labelling, Como's **Pinacoteca Civica** (📞031 26 98 69; Via Diaz 84; adult/reduced €4/2; ⏰10am-6pm Tue-Sun) has a sizeable collection with some rich pickings. Most interesting are the frescoes and sculpture from the convent of Santa Margherita, the collection of Renaissance portraits donated by Paolo Giovio, and the surprising 19th-century galleries on the top floor. The latter are dedicated to the work of rationalist architect Antonio Sant'Elia and the Como Group, including Manlio Rho, who is widely considered one of the best abstract artists in Italy.

# Survival Guide

View of the city from the Duomo (p32) STEFANO BERTELLI/500PX ©

# Before You Go

## Book Your Stay

Finding a room in Milan isn't easy, particularly during trade fairs and fashion weeks when rates skyrocket. Services you'd take for granted elsewhere, such as breakfast or wi-fi, sometimes command an extra fee. That said, booking ahead and comparison-shopping online for 'special rates' can result in unexpected deals.

## Useful Websites

**Cenacolo Vinciano** (www.cenacolovinciano.org) Booking for *The Last Supper*, which is handled by Vivatickets.

**Hello Milano** (www.hellomilano.it) English-language website with information on events, exhibitions and concerts.

**Lonely Planet** (www.lonelyplanet.com/milan) Destination information, hotel

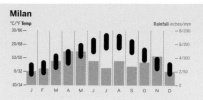

## When to Go

o **Mar–Jun** Peak season; the Furniture Fair and Fashion Weeks are in progress.

o **Jul–Aug** Low season; Milan is sweltering so everyone heads to the lakes.

o **Sep–Oct** Football season, new exhibitions and autumn fashion shows.

o **Nov–Feb** The Feast of St Ambrose, start of opera season; Christmas fairs; January sales and Carnival.

bookings, traveller forum and more.

**Milan Tourism** (www.turismo.milano.it; www.yesmilano.it) Milan's excellent official tourism portals.

**Vivi Milano** (http://vivimilano.corriere.it) Restaurant and cultural listings from newspaper *Corriere della Sera*.

**Dissapore** (www.dissapore.com) One-stop food hub with opinionated news and reviews.

## Best Budget

**Babila Hostel** ( 02 3658 8490; www.babilahostel.it; Via Conservatorio 2a; dm €30-42, d/qd €89-

159/120-176; ❄ 🛜; Ⓜ San Babila) Hostel living in grand Gothic style.

**Casa Base** (http://base.milano.it; Via Bergognone 34; dm with/without bathroom €55/35, d €90-120; ❄ 🛜; Ⓜ Porta Genova) Funky 1950s, Stella Orsini design on a budget.

**Ostello Bello** ( 02 3658 2720; www.ostellobello.com; Via Medici 4; dm/d €47/159; ❄ 🛜 🍴; 🚊 2, 3, 14) A bargain with a terrace and bar.

## Best Midrange

**Maison Borella** ( 02 5810 9114; www.hotelmaisonborella.com; Alzaia Naviglio Grande 8; d €170-255;

classy, period renova-
tion that out-does
grander neighbours.

**Atellani Apartments**
( ☎ 340 951 91 26; www.
atellaniapartments.com;
Corso Magenta 65; 1-bed
apt €157-228, 2-bed apt
€218-332; P ☎ ; ⛁16)
Lay your head where
da Vinci once did in the
Atellani palace.

**Foresteria Un Posto a
Milano** ( ☎ 02 545 7785;
www.unpostoamilano.it;
Via Cuccagna 2; s €70-115,
d €90-144, qd €284; ☎ ;
M Porta Romana) Family-
friendly, farm stay–
style accommodation
with a large garden.

## Best Top End

**Palazzo Parigi** ( ☎ 02 62
56 25; www.palazzoparigi.
com; Corso di Porta Nuova
1; d/ste €450-700/610-
2800; P ❄ ☎ ⛱ ;
M Turati) Old-school
Parisian glamour that
serves as an antidote to
all the edginess.

**Bulgari Hotel**
( ☎ 02 805 80 51; www.
bulgarihotels.com; Via
Privata Fratelli Gabba 7b; d
€720-920, ste €990-2900;
P ❄ @ ☎ ⛱ ; M Mon-
tenapoleone) A favourite
with the fashion pack.

# Arriving in Milan

## Malpensa Airport

Northern Italy's main
international airport,
**Malpensa** (MXP; ☎ 02 23
23 23; www.milanomalpensa
-airport.com; ☒ Malpensa
Express), is located 50km
northwest of Milan.

Terminal 1 receives
the majority of sched-
uled international and
domestic flights, while
Terminal 2 is dedicated
to low-cost carriers
such as EasyJet.

A free shuttle con-
nects Terminal 1 and
Terminal 2.

**Train** The Malpensa
Express runs from both
airport terminals to the
city centre (50 minutes)
every 30 minutes from
5.50am to 12.20am.

**Bus** The Malpensa
Shuttle runs a lim-
ited service between
12.20am and 5.50am.

**Taxis** A cab into central
Milan is €90 set fare
(50 minutes).

## Linate Airport

The more convenient
**Linate Airport** (LIN;

☎ 02 23 23 23; www.
milanolinate-airport.com;
Viale Enrico Forlanini), 7km
east of the city centre,
handles the majority of
domestic and a hand-
ful of European flights.

**Bus** Airport Bus
Express run coaches to
Stazione Centrale (25
minutes) every 30 min-
utes between 5.30am
and 10pm; Air Bus of-
fers a similar service.

**City Bus** ATM bus
number 73 departs to
Via Gonzaga (€1.50,
25 minutes) every
10-20 minutes between
5.35am and 12.35am.

**Taxis** cost between
€20 and €30, depend-
ing on your destination.

## Stazione Centrale

Milan's monumental
**Stazione Centrale**
(www.milanocentrale.
it; Piazza Duca d'Aosta;
🕑 4am-1am; M Centrale)
receives international,
high-speed trains from
France, Switzerland,
Austria and Germany.

The ticketing office
and left luggage are
located on the ground
floor. For domestic ser-
vices, skip the queue
and buy your tickets
from the multilingual,

touch-screen vending machines, which accept both cash and credit card.

High-speed *Freccia* and *Italo* trains that serve major Italian cities have their own information lounge.

# Getting Around

## Bicycle

o Both **Mobike** (https://mobike.com) and **ofo** (http://ofo.com) offer dockless bike sharing through their apps.

o Alternatively, **BikeMi** (☑ 02 4860 7607; www.bikemi.it) is a public bicycle system with stops all over town. Subscribe and register for all services online or through their apps. For BikeMi you can also register at the **ATM Info Point** (Azienda Trasporti Milano; ☑ 02 4860 7607; www.atm.it) at

the Duomo, Cadorna or Centrale metro stops.

## Metro

o **ATM** (Azienda Trasporti Milano; ☑ 02 4860 7607; www.atm.it) runs Milan's public transport network, including the metro.

o Services operate between 5.40am and 12.20am (from 6.15am on Sunday).

o There are four lines: M1 (red) connects Duomo with Porta Venezia, the castle, Corso Magenta and the Fiera; M2 (green) connects Porta Garibaldi with Brera and Navigli; M3 (yellow) connects the Quad with Porta Romana; and, M5 (lilac) connects San Siro with Porta Garibaldi and Isola.

o Work is well underway on the M4 (blue) line, after many delays. It will connect the city with Linate Airport.

o A ticket costs €1.50 and is valid for one metro ride. Tickets are sold at elec-

tronic ticket machines in the station, or at tobacconists and newsstands.

o Download the free ATM app for network maps and timetables.

## Tram & Bus

o **ATM** (Azienda Trasporti Milano; ☑ 02 4860 7607; www.atm.it) also oversees trams and an extensive bus network.

o Route maps are available from ATM info points, or download the ATM app.

o Tickets are sold at electronic ticket machines in the station, or at tobacconists and newsstands.

o A ticket costs €1.50 and is valid for 90 minutes on trams and buses. It must be validated when boarding.

o Tram 1, which cuts through the historic centre, is a retro orange beauty with wooden benches and original fittings.

o Trams 2 and 3 are good for sightseeing, and trams 9 and 10 loop the whole way around the centre via Porta Venezia, Porta Genova and Porta Garibaldi.

o Bus-based night services run every half-hour

## Bike Hire

Consider renting one from **Rossignoli** (☑ 02 80 49 60; www.rossignoli.it; Corso Garibaldi 71; bike rental 1 day/week €12/65; ⏰ 2.30-7.30pm Mon, 9am-12.30pm & 2.30-7.30pm Tue-Sat; M Moscova), Milan's oldest bike outfit.

between 12.20am and 5.40am, when the metro is closed.

## Taxi

o Taxis cannot be hailed but must be picked up at designated ranks, usually outside train stations, large hotels and in major piazzas.

o You can call a cab on 📞02 40 40, 📞02 69 69 or 📞02 85 85.

o Be aware that when you call for a cab, the meter runs from receipt of the call, not pickup.

o The average short city ride costs €10.

o There's a fixed rate price for the airports.

# Essential Information

## Accessible Travel

Milan is the only Italian city with a stated policy of becoming accessible to all. That said there's still a long way to go and getting around can be challenging for the wheelchair-bound.

### Useful Tickets & Passes

There are several good money-saving passes available for public transport:

**One-day ticket** Valid for 24 hours; €4.50

**Two-day ticket** Valid for 48 hours; €8.25

**Carnet of 10 tickets** Valid for 90 minutes each; €13.80

**Evening ticket** Valid from 8pm until the end of service; €3

For those with limited mobility, the public transport operator **ATM** (Azienda Trasporti Milano; 📞02 4860 7607; www.atm.it) has introduced low-floor buses on many of its routes, and some metro stations are now equipped with suitable lifts. See the dual-language **Milano Per Tutti** (www.milanopertutti.it) for details and for itineraries of accessible sights.

Download Lonely Planet's free *Accessible Travel* guides from http://lptravel.to/AccessibleTravel.

## Business Hours

Opening hours are longer in summer. Many shops and restaurants close for several weeks during August, or have reduced hours.

**Banks** 8.30am–1.30pm and 3.30–4.30pm Monday to Friday

**Bars & clubs** 10pm–4am; may open earlier if they have restaurants

**Cafes** 7.30am–8pm; most serve alcoholic drinks in the evening

**Restaurants** noon–2.30pm and 7.30–11pm; often later in summer; most close one day a week

**Shops** 9am–1pm and 3.30–7.30pm (or 4–8pm) Monday to Saturday; larger shops stay open over lunchtime, and also on Sundays

## Discount Cards

**Civic Museum Card** (€12; www.turismo.milano.it) This three-day ticket allows a single admission to each of Milan's nine civic museums. Tickets can be purchased online or at any of the museums.

**House Museums Card** (adult/reduced €20/10; www.casemu seo.it) Gives discounted access to Milan's four house museums. It's valid for six months and can be purchased at any of the houses.

## Electricity

Type F
230V/50Hz

## Emergency

| | |
|---|---|
| Italy's country code | ☎ 39 |
| Milan city code | ☎ 02 |
| Ambulance | ☎ 112 |
| Police | ☎ 112 |
| Fire | ☎ 115 |

## Money

ATMs are widely available. To change money, you'll need to present your passport ID.

### Credit Cards

Visa and MasterCard are among the most widely recognised, but others such as Cirrus and Maestro are also accepted. American Express and Diners Club are not universally accepted, so check in advance.

### Tipping

Tipping is not generally expected nor demanded in Italy as it is in some other countries. This said, a discretionary tip for good service is appreciated in some circumstances.

Use the following as a guide:

**Top-end hotel** Tip at least €2, for porter, maid or room service.

**Restaurant** If service isn't included on the bill, leave a 10% to 15% tip.

**Bar** Most Italians just leave small change (€0.10 to €0.20 is fine).

**Taxi** Not normal prac-

tice, although locals usually round up to the nearest euro.

## Public Holidays

Banks, offices and some shops will close on public holidays. Restaurants, museums and tourist attractions tend to stay open.

**New Year's Day** (Capodanno or Anno Nuovo) 1 January

**Epiphany** (Epifania) 6 January

**Easter Monday** (Pasquetta) March/April

**Liberation Day** (Giorno della Liberazione) 25 April

**Labour Day** (Festa del Lavoro) 1 May

**Republic Day** (Festa della Repubblica) 2 June

**Feast of the Assumption** (Assunzione or Ferragosto) 15 August

**All Saints Day** (Ognissanti) 1 November

**Patron Saint Day** (Festa di Sant'Ambrogio) 7 December

**Feast of the Immaculate Conception** (Immacolata Concezione) 8 December

**Christmas Day** (Natale) 25 December

**Boxing Day** (Festa di San Stefano) 26 December

## Safe Travel

o Milan is a safe and affluent destination; however, as with any major city, pickpocketing can be an issue at busy train stations and Piazza del Duomo.

o A Green Pass (EU COVID-19 certificate) is essential to visit all tourist sites in Italy. For up-to-date information on COVID-19 protocols in Milan and Lombardy, refer to www.yesmilano.it.

## Telephone

The dialling code for Italy is 39 and the city code for Milan is 02. The city code is an integral part of the number and must always be dialled. Toll-free (free-phone) numbers, known as *numeri verdi*, start with 800.

## Mobile Phones

o Italy uses GSM 900/1800, which is compatible with the rest of Europe and Australia but not with North American GSM 1900 or the Japanese system.

o There are no roaming charges within the European Union.

o To buy a SIM card you'll need your passport and the address of your accommodation.

## Tourist Information

**Milan Tourist Office** (Map p38, C2; ☎ 02 8845 5555; www.turismo.milano.it; Galleria Vittorio Emanuele II 11-12; ⏰ 9am-7pm Mon-Fri, to 6pm Sat, 10am-6pm Sun; M Duomo) Centrally located in the Galleria, with helpful English-speaking staff and lots of maps and information on exhibitions and events.

# Responsible Travel

## Overtourism

o Visit www.yesmilano.it for information on Milan's sustainable efforts and some great walking and cycling itineraries.

o Pre-book visits to the Duomo, Pinacoteca di Brera and the *Last Supper*.

o Walk or use the public transport system, which extends to Lake Como, Lake Maggiore and Pavia.

o Explore beyond the centre and along canal paths into the countryside.

## Support Local

o Stay in ecofriendly hotels such as Milano Scala, E.c.h.o and Foresteria Un Posto a Milano; and check any rented accommodation is registered.

o Shop at the market, especially Mercato di Porta Romana.

o Visit sustainable food champions at Eataly, Mercato Comunale and Joia.

## Light Footprint

o Order tap water and carry your own water bottle.

o Avail of the 4500 public bikes or scooters.

o Shop vintage stores such as Cavalli e Nastri, BIVIO, SNAP, Vintage Delirium and the East Market.

o Milan is a major European rail hub: arrive by train if you can.

# Language

Standard Italian is taught and spoken throughout Italy. Regional dialects are an important part of identity in many parts of the country, but you'll have no trouble being understood anywhere if you stick to standard Italian, which we've also used in this chapter.

The sounds used in spoken Italian can all be found in English. If you read our pronunciation guides as if they were English, you'll be understood. The stressed syllables are indicated with italics. Note that *ai* is pronounced as in 'aisle', *ay* as in 'say', *ow* as in 'how', *dz* as the 'ds' in 'lids', and that *r* is a strong, rolled sound.

To enhance your trip with a phrasebook, visit lonelyplanet.com.

## Basics

**Hello.**
*Buongiorno.*    bwon·*jor*·no

**Goodbye.**
*Arrivederci.*    a·ree·ve·*der*·chee

**How are you?**
*Come sta?*    *ko*·me sta

**Fine. And you?**
*Bene. E Lei?*    *be*·ne e lay

**Please.**
*Per favore.*    per fa·*vo*·re

**Thank you.**
*Grazie.*    *gra*·tsye

**Excuse me.**
*Mi scusi.*    mee *skoo*·zee

**Sorry.**
*Mi dispiace.*    mee dees·*pya*·che

**Yes./No.**
*Sì./No.*    see/no

**I don't understand.**
*Non capisco.*    non ka·*pee*·sko

**Do you speak English?**
*Parla inglese?*    *par*·la een·*gle*·ze

## Eating & Drinking

**I'd like ...**    *Vorrei ...*    vo·*ray* ..
    **a coffee**    *un caffè*    oon ka·*fe*
    **a table**    *un tavolo*    oon *ta*·vo·lo
    **the menu**    *il menù*    eel me·*noo*
    **two beers**    *due birre*    doo·e *bee*·re

**What would you recommend?**
*Cosa mi*    *ko*·za mee
*consiglia?*    kon·*see*·lya

**Enjoy the meal!**
*Buon appetito!*    bwon a·pe·*tee*·to

**That was delicious!**
*Era squisito!*    *e*·ra skwee·zee·to

**Cheers!**
*Salute!*    sa·*loo*·te

**Please bring the bill.**
*Mi porta il*    mee *por*·ta eel
*conto, per favore?*    *kon* to per fa·*vo*·re

## Shopping

**I'd like to buy ...**
*Vorrei comprare ...*    vo·*ray* kom·*pra*·re ...

**I'm just looking.**
*Sto solo*    sto *so*·lo
*guardando.*    gwar·*dan*·do

## How much is this?

*Quanto costa questo?* — kwan·to kos·ta kwe·sto

## It's too expensive.

*È troppo caro/cara. (m/f)* — e tro·po ka·ro/ka·ra

## Emergencies

### Help!
*Aiuto!* — a·yoo·to

### Call the police!
*Chiami la polizia!* — kya·mee la po·lee·tsee·a

### Call a doctor!
*Chiami un medico!* — kya·mee oon me·dee·ko

### I'm sick.
*Mi sento male.* — mee sen·to ma·le

### I'm lost.
*Mi sono perso/persa. (m/f)* — mee so·no per·so/per·sa

### Where are the toilets?
*Dove sono i gabinetti?* — do·ve so·no ee ga·bee·ne·tee

## Time & Numbers

### What time is it?
*Che ora è?* — ke o·ra e

### It's (two) o'clock.
*Sono le (due).* — so·no le (doo·e)

| | | |
|---|---|---|
| morning | *mattina* | ma·tee·na |
| afternoon | *pomeriggio* | po·me·ree·jo |
| evening | *sera* | se·ra |
| yesterday | *ieri* | ye·ree |
| today | *oggi* | o·jee |
| tomorrow | *domani* | do·ma·nee |

| | | |
|---|---|---|
| 1 | *uno* | oo·no |
| 2 | *due* | doo·e |
| 3 | *tre* | tre |
| 4 | *quattro* | kwa·tro |
| 5 | *cinque* | cheen·kwe |
| 6 | *sei* | say |
| 7 | *sette* | se·te |
| 8 | *otto* | o·to |
| 9 | *nove* | no·ve |
| 10 | *dieci* | dye·chee |
| 100 | *cento* | chen·to |
| 1000 | *mille* | mee·le |

## Transport & Directions

### Where's ...?
*Dov'è ...?* — do·ve ...

### What's the address?
*Qual'è l'indirizzo?* — kwa·le leen·dee·ree·tso

### Can you show me (on the map)?
*Può mostrarmi (sulla pianta)?* — pwo mos·trar·mee (soo·la pyan·ta)

### At what time does the ... leave?
*A che ora parte ...?* — a ke o·ra par·te

### Does it stop at ...?
*Si ferma a ...?* — see fer·ma a ...

### How do I get there?
*Come ci si arriva?* — ko·me chee see a·ree·va

| | | |
|---|---|---|
| bus | *l'autobus* | low·to·boos |
| ticket | *un biglietto* | oon bee·lye·to |
| timetable | *orario* | o·ra·ryo |
| train | *il treno* | eel tre·no |

# Behind the Scenes

## Send Us Your Feedback

We love to hear from travellers – your comments help make our books better. We read every word, and we guarantee that your feedback goes straight to the authors. Visit **lonelyplanet.com/contact** to submit your updates and suggestions.

Note: We may edit, reproduce and incorporate your comments in Lonely Planet products such as guidebooks, websites and digital products, so let us know if you don't want your comments reproduced or your name acknowledged. For a copy of our privacy policy visit lonelyplanet.com/legal.

## Paula's Thanks

*Grazie mille* to all the fun and fashionable Milanese who spilled the beans on their remarkable city: Paola dalla Valentina, Luisa Zanardi, Claudio Galimberti, Isabella Menichini, Serena Tagliabue, Costanza Cecchini, Marco Rivolta and Federica at the Como Tourist Office. Special thanks also to Director Martinazzoli for his time and insights. Thanks, too, to Rob for sharing life on the road.

## Acknowledgements

Cover photographs: (front) Duomo di Milano (Milan Cathedral), Martin Wahlborg/Getty Images ©; (back) Bar Basso, Milan, Matt Munro/LP Traveller Magazine ©

Photographs pp26–7 (from top): Matej Kastelic, Nadia Mikushova/ Shutterstock ©

## This Book

This 5th edition of Lonely Planet's *Pocket Milan* guidebook was researched and written by Paula Hardy, who also wrote the previous three editions. This guidebook was produced by the following:

**Destination Editor**
Anna Tyler

**Senior Product Editors**
Sandie Kestell, Elizabeth Jones

**Product Editors** Kirsten Rawlings, Kate Kiely

**Senior Cartographers**
Julie Sheridan, Anthony Phelan

**Book Designers** Hannah Blackie, Mazzy Prinsep

**Assisting Editors** Emma Gibbs, Victoria Harrison, Jodie Martire, Anne Mulvaney

**Cartographer**
Julie Dodkins

**Cover Researcher**
Kat Marsh

**Thanks to** Ronan Abayawickrema, Camilla Jensen, Sonia Kapoor, Stephanie Ong

# Index

See also separate subindexes for:

⊗ **Eating p157**
⊙ **Drinking p158**
⊗ **Entertainment p158**
⊙ **Shopping p159**

Sights 000
Map Pages **000**

## ⊗ Eating

# ⓐ Shopping

# Our Writer

### Paula Hardy

Paula Hardy is an independent travel writer and editorial consultant, whose work for Lonely Planet and other flagship publications has taken her from nomadic camps in the Danakil Depression to Seychellois beach huts and the jewel-like bar at the Gritti Palace on the Grand Canal. Over two decades, she has authored more than 30 Lonely Planet guidebooks and spent five years as commissioning editor of Lonely Planet's bestselling Italian list. These days you'll find her hunting down new hotels, hip bars and up-and-coming artisans primarily in Milan, Venice and Marrakesh. Get in touch at www.paulahardy.com.

**Published by Lonely Planet Global Limited**
CRN 554153
5th edition – Mar 2022
ISBN 978 1 78868 040 0
© Lonely Planet 2022   Photographs © as indicated 2022
10 9 8 7 6 5 4
Printed in Malaysia

# Explore ◈
# City Centre
# & Haymarket

*Occupying a rough grid pattern south of the Rocks, Sydney's central business district (CBD) offers upmarket shopping, eating and sightseeing, with gracious colonial buildings scattered among the skyscrapers and orderly parks providing breathing space. The breathless jumble of Haymarket and Chinatown provides a chaotic contrast.*

*Sydney's towering central business district (CBD) encapsulates the city's cavalier spirit, with skyscrapers unashamedly overshadowing historic sandstone buildings and churches.*

*While pacing the grid of central streets gives a good idea of contemporary corporate Sydney, it's worth identifying a few key spots of interest before plunging into the urban jungle. Make sure to dedicate a little time to strolling Hyde Park and the array of historic buildings along Macquarie Street.*

## Getting There & Around

🚆 Train is the best option for getting here, with six stations.

🚌 There are numerous bus lines, with major nodes at Wynyard Park, the QVB and Central station (Railway Sq).

🚊 Three light rail lines. The L1 will take you to Central from the west, while the L2 and L3 both run the length of the CBD along George St, from Circular Quay to Central before heading out to the southeast.

### City Centre & Haymarket Map on p62

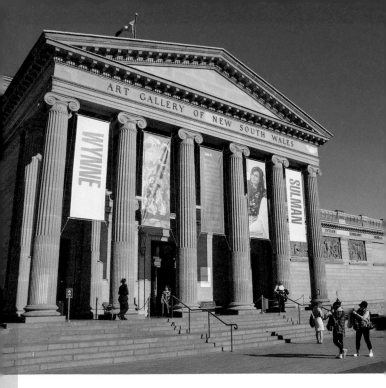

## Top Experience 📷
# Discover Amazing Art at the Art Gallery of NSW

*The city's major gallery is a cornerstone of Sydney life. While locals throng to the major touring exhibitions, the main attraction here is the outstanding assemblage of Indigenous and colonial Australian art. There's also a lively line-up of cultural events and children's activities. An expansion is due to add a modern annex, Sydney Modern, scheduled for completion in 2022.*

◉ MAP P62, F3

☎ 1800 679 278

www.artgallery.nsw.gov.au

Art Gallery Rd

admission free

🕙 10am-5pm Thu-Tue, to 10pm Wed

🚌 441, 🚇 St James

## The Collection

While the permanent collection has a strong collection of 19th-century European and Australian art, the highlights are the contemporary Indigenous gallery in the basement, and the collection of 20th-century Australian art, with some standout canvases by the big names of the local painting scene. Look out for Albert Tucker's scary *Apocalyptic Horse*, Russell Drysdale's brilliant gold-town street *Sofala* and half a room of Sidney Nolans, usually including one or more of his extraordinary Ned Kelly paintings. There's a good representation of female artists too, including Grace Cossington Smith and several Margaret Olleys on rotation. Arthur Boyd works include his terracotta sculpture of *Judas Kissing Christ*, while Brett Whiteley is represented by the intoxicatingly blue harbour of *The Balcony 2*.

## Prizes

The $100,000 **Archibald Prize** for portraiture is a much-talked-about Sydney event that garners attention with its lure of celebrity subjects. It's so popular that it's generated three spin-offs: the Salon des Refusés at the SH Ervin Gallery (p42); the highly irreverent Bald Archies; and the Packing Room Prize (judged by the employees who unload the crates).

The $50,000 **Wynne Prize** for landscape painting or figure sculpture and the $40,000 **Sir John Sulman Prize** for subject or mural painting don't usually cause as much consternation.

## New Developments

Construction of a second building was approved in 2017 and is due to be completed in 2022. Occupying space to the north of the existing building, it's a major project, to be known as Sydney Modern, that will be centred around a new Indigenous gallery and a dedicated space for major touring exhibitions. The construction work shouldn't affect gallery visits.

### ★ Top Tips

○ Major exhibitions absolutely pack out at weekends, so try and visit midweek if Picasso or Van Gogh are in town.

○ Check the gallery website before you visit, as all sorts of activities and events are often on.

### ✗ Take a Break

The gallery's **restaurant** (☏ 02-9225 1819; www.chiswick restaurant.com.au; Art Gallery Rd; small plates $19-25, mains $29-40; ☺ noon-3.30pm Thu-Tue, to 9pm Wed; ☎ ), on the entrance level, and **cafe**, a floor down, are pleasant spaces with outdoor seating and harbour views.

Wander down to Woolloomooloo Bay for a pie at Harry's Cafe de Wheels (p136) or upmarket harbourside Italian at Otto (p139).

City Centre & Haymarket Discover Amazing Art at the Art Gallery of NSW

## Top Experience 📷
# Eat Your Fill in Chinatown

*Wedged into the Haymarket district, Sydney's Chinatown is a tight nest of restaurants, food courts, shops and aroma-filled alleyways, centred on Dixon St. No longer just Chinese, the area is truly pan-Asian. Head here for cheap eats any time of the day or night.*

◎ MAP P62, B7

www.sydney-chinatown.info

🚋 Paddy's Markets,
🚆 Town Hall

## Dixon Street

Dixon St is the heart of Chinatown: a narrow, shady pedestrian mall with a string of restaurants and insistent spruikers. The ornate dragon gates (*paifang*) at either end have fake bamboo tiles, golden Chinese calligraphy and ornamental lions to keep evil spirits at bay.

This is actually Sydney's third Chinatown: the first was in the Rocks in the late 19th century before it moved to the Darling Harbour end of Market St. Dixon St's Chinatown dates from the 1920s. Look for the fake-bamboo awnings guarded by dragons, dogs and lions, and kooky upturned-wok lighting fixtures.

## Other Areas

On Chinatown's western border, the Chinese Garden of Friendship (pictured; p79) is a peaceful oasis, while on Hay St, the Golden Water Mouth sculpture represents a symbolic fusion of China and Australia. A little further down Hay St, Paddy's Markets (p75) fills the lower level of a hefty brick building. It started out in the mid-19th century with mainly European traders, but these days the tightly packed market stalls are more evocative of present-day Vietnam.

## Eating

Chinatown in general (not necessarily just between the dragon gates) is a fabulous eating district, which effectively extends for several blocks north and south of Dixon Street. Beyond Paddy's Markets, there's some great cheap eating to be done in the area around Thomas and Quay Streets and Ultimo Road. To the east, across George Street, Chinatown segues into Koreatown and Thaitown, with more great eateries.

### ★ Top Tips

o It's worth visiting twice: once during the day to see the bustle of the markets and shops, and again after dark for the all-night buzz.

o Though it's got the dragon gates, Dixon Street is arguably the least interesting part of Chinatown: make sure you explore further.

### ✗ Take a Break

The area's food courts hide numerous quality noodle outlets. Gumshara (p67) does legendary ramen.

For a traditional and upmarket Chinese dining experience, check in to Golden Century (p71). Order seafood.

# Walking Tour 🚶

# City Escapes

*Sydney's two most imposing streets are Macquarie St, the centre of government, and intersecting with it, Martin Place, its financial heart. During weekdays they thrum to the beat of politics and commerce. When the daily hustle gets too much, bureaucrats and office workers seek sanctuary in the inner city's parks or head to Pitt Street Mall for some shopfront fantasies.*

## Walk Facts

**Start** The Domain

**End** Hyde Park

**Length** 2.5km, one to two hours

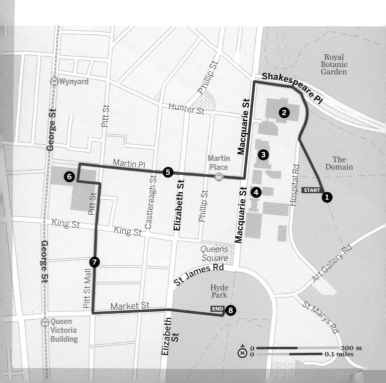

## ❶ Dawdle Through the Domain

This large **grassy tract** (www.rbgsyd.nsw.gov.au; Art Gallery Rd; 🚇St James) was set aside by Governor Phillip in 1788 for public recreation. Today's city workers use the space to work up a sweat or eat their lunch. Large-scale public events are also held here.

## ❷ Study the State Library

Scholars sneak off to the elegant main reading room of the **State Library of NSW** (🕿02-9273 1414; www.sl.nsw.gov.au; Macquarie St; admission free; 🕘9am-8pm Mon-Thu, to 5pm Fri, 10am-5pm Sat & Sun; 🚇Martin Place) seeking inspiration within its milky marble walls. The library holds more than five million tomes and good temporary exhibitions.

## ❸ Visit the People's Place

Built in 1816 as part of the Rum Hospital, **Parliament House** (🕿02-9230 2111; www.parliament.nsw.gov.au; 6 Macquarie St; admission free; 🕘9am-5pm Mon-Fri; 🚇Martin Place) has been home to the Parliament of New South Wales since 1829, making it the world's oldest continually operating parliament building. Everyone's welcome to visit the assembly chambers, art exhibitions and historical displays.

## ❹ Sydney Hospital

Australia's oldest **hospital** (8 Macquarie St; 🚇Martin Place) has a grand Victorian sandstone facade and a peaceful central courtyard

with a cafe. In provocative recline out the front of the hospital is the pig-ugly bronze statue Il Porcellino. Rub its snout for luck.

## ❺ March Down Martin Place

Studded with imposing edifices, **Martin Place** (🚇Wynyard, 🚇Martin Place) was closed to traffic in 1971, forming a pedestrian mall. It's the closest thing to a town square that Sydney has. Near the George St end is the Cenotaph, commemorating Australia's war dead.

## ❻ Rehydrate in GPO Sydney

As iconic as the Opera House in its time (1874), the **General Post Office** (GPO; www.gpogrand.com; 1 Martin Pl; 🚇Wynyard, 🚇Martin Place), a colonnaded Victorian palazzo, has been gutted, stabbed with office towers and transformed into a hotel, restaurants and bars.

## ❼ Pitt Street Mall Shopping

As you sidestep the buskers on this car-free shopping street, look out for the Strand Arcade on your right and Westfield Sydney on your left.

## ❽ Hang Out in Hyde Park

Formal but much-loved **Hyde Park** (Elizabeth St; 🚇St James, Museum) has manicured gardens and a tree-formed tunnel running down its spine. The park's northern end is crowned by the richly symbolic art deco **Archibald Memorial Fountain**, featuring Greek mythological figures, while at the other end is the **Anzac Memorial**.

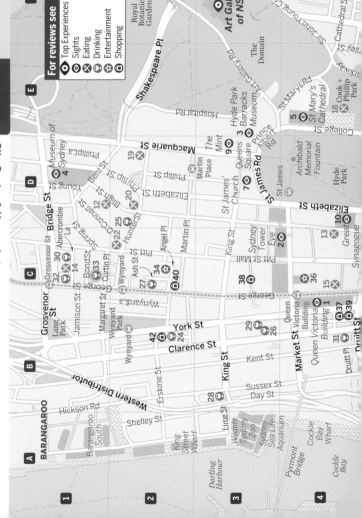

**For reviews see**

| | | |
|---|---|---|
| ● | Top Experiences | p56 |
| ◉ | Sights | p64 |
| ✕ | Eating | p67 |
| 🍷 | Drinking | p71 |
| 🎭 | Entertainment | p73 |
| 🛍 | Shopping | p74 |

Royal Botanic Garden

Art Gallery of NSW

The Domain

Sir John Young Cres

Cathedral St

...ley St

...kway

18 Cook + Phillip Park

Shakespeare Pl

Hospital Rd

Art Gallery Rd

St Marys Rd

St Mary's Cathedral

College St

Hyde Park Barracks Museum

5

Archibald Memorial Fountain

Hyde Park

Museum of Sydney

4

Phillip La

Macquarie St

The Mint

9

Prince Albert Rd

Young St

Bent St

19

Martin Place

Queens Square

3

Bligh St

Phillip St

Elizabeth St

St James' Church

7

Queens Square

St James

Elizabeth St

Bridge St

Grosvenor St

Abercrombie

La

12

20

O'Connell St

Hunter St

Martin Pl

King St

Sydney Tower Eye

2

10

Great...

Synagogue

13

Grosvenor St

32 30

Spring St

22 25

14

33

Curtin Pl

BondSt

27

Ash St

Angel Pl

34

Pitt St Mall

Sydney Tower Eye

40

38

Pitt St

36

15

Lang Park

Jamison St

Margaret St

Wynyard Park

Wynyard

George St

George St

Wynyard La

Queen

Market St

Queen Victoria Building

37

39

31

Druitt Pl

Druitt St

Grosvenor St

Wynyard

York St

Clarence St

42

24

29

26

King St

Kent St

Queen Victoria Building

1

Victoria Building

BARANGAROO

Western Distributor

Hickson Rd

Shelley St

Erskine St

Sussex St

Day St

28

Lime St

King Street Wharf

Barangaroo South

Wildlife Sydney Zoo

Sydney Sea Life Aquarium

Darling Harbour

Pyrmont Bridge

Cockle Bay Wharf

Cockle Bay

# Sights

## Queen Victoria Building
HISTORIC BUILDING

**1** 👁 MAP P62, C4

Unbelievably, this High Victorian Gothic masterpiece (1898) was repeatedly slated for demolition before it was restored in the 1980s. Occupying an entire city block on the site of the city's first markets, it is a Venetian Romanesque–inspired temple to the gods of retail. (QVB; 📞02-9264 9209; www.qvb.com.au; 455 George St; tours $15; ⏰9am-6pm Mon-Wed, Fri & Sat, 9am-9pm Thu, 11am-5pm Sun; 🚈Town Hall)

## Sydney Tower Eye
TOWER

**2** 👁 MAP P62, C4

The 309m-tall Sydney Tower (finished in 1981 and still known as Centrepoint by many Sydneysiders) offers unbeatable 360-degree views from the observation level 250m up – and even better ones for the daredevils braving the Skywalk on its roof. The visit starts with the 4D Experience, a short 3D film giving you a bird's-eye view (a parakeet's to be exact) of city, surf, harbour and what lies beneath the water, accompanied by mist sprays and bubbles – it's actually pretty darn cool.

Luke Skywalker aspirations? Don a spiffy 'skysuit' and take the **Skywalk**: shackle yourself to the safety rail and step onto two glass-floored viewing platforms outside Sydney Tower's observation deck, 268m above the street. It's no place

for the weak-bowelled. Tickets are cheaper online, or as part of a Sydney Attractions Pass. The entrance is on the 5th floor of the **Westfield shopping centre** (📞02-8236 9200; www.westfield.com.au/sydney; ⏰9.30am-7pm Mon-Wed, Fri & Sat, to 9pm Thu, 10am-7pm Sun; 🛜), near the food court but surprisingly poorly signposted. There are two revolving restaurants: an extremely mediocre buffet and a somewhat better fine-dining establishment. In the revolving dining stakes, O Bar (p73) in the Australia Square building is a better bet. (www.sydneytowereye.com.au; Level 5, Westfield Sydney, 188 Pitt St; adult/child $28/19, Skywalk $70/49; ⏰9am-9.30pm May-Sep, to 10pm Oct-Apr; 🚈St James)

## Hyde Park Barracks Museum
MUSEUM

**3** 👁 MAP P62, E3

Convict architect Francis Greenway designed this squarish, decorously Georgian structure (1819) as convict quarters. Fifty thousand men and boys sentenced to transportation passed through here in 30 years. It later became an immigration depot, a women's asylum and a law court. These days it's a fascinating museum, focusing on the barracks' history and the archaeological efforts that helped reveal it. The top floor has hammocks strung out as they were back in the day. Entry includes a good audio guide. (📞02-8239 2311; www.sydneylivingmuseums.com.au; Queens Sq, Macquarie St; adult/child $12/8; ⏰10am-5pm; 🚈St James)